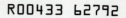

Groundwater Pollution

Environmental and Legal Problems

AAAS Selected Symposia Series

 Published by Westview Press, Inc.
5500 Central Avenue, Boulder, Colorado

for the

American Association for the Advancement of Science
1776 Massachusetts Ave., N.W., Washington, D.C.

Groundwater Pollution

Environmental and Legal Problems

*Edited by Curtis C. Travis
and Elizabeth L. Etnier*

AAAS Selected Symposium **95**

AAAS Selected Symposia Series

This book is based on a symposium that was held at the 1982 AAAS National
Annual Meeting in Washington, D.C., January 3-8. The symposium was sponsored
by AAAS Section X (General).

Published in 1984 in the United States of America by Westview Press, Inc.,
5500 Central Avenue, Boulder, Colorado 80301; Frederick A. Praeger, President
and Publisher

Library of Congress Catalog Card Number: 84-50534
ISBN: 0-8133-0001-0

Printed and bound in the United States of America

10 9 8 7 6 5 4 3 2 1

BST
R

About the Book

The pollution of our nation's groundwater supplies is causing increasing concern among scientists, legislators, and the public. Although traditionally surface water has been considered to be much more susceptible to contamination, recent analysis indicates that many of our groundwater aquifers have also been contaminated by a variety of synthetic organic compounds; and until the long-term health effects of low-level exposure to these compounds are known, their presence in groundwater must be considered a significant threat to human health. This book highlights the methodological and conceptual difficulties inherent in protecting the nation's groundwater supplies and provides up-to-date information on groundwater hydrology, the nature and extent of the groundwater pollution problem, and the possible effects of exposure to contaminated drinking water. The authors provide insight into the difficult legal issues involved in protecting groundwater quality and stress the need for a comprehensive federal and state groundwater protection program.

About the Series

The *AAAS Selected Symposia Series* was begun in 1977 to provide a means for more permanently recording and more widely disseminating some of the valuable material which is discussed at the AAAS Annual National Meetings. The volumes in this *Series* are based on symposia held at the Meetings which address topics of current and continuing significance, both within and among the sciences, and in the areas in which science and technology impact on public policy. The *Series* format is designed to provide for rapid dissemination of information, so the papers are not typeset but are reproduced directly from the camera-copy submitted by the authors. The papers are organized and edited by the symposium arrangers who then become the editors of the various volumes. Most papers published in this *Series* are original contributions which have not been previously published, although in some cases additional papers from other sources have been added by an editor to provide a more comprehensive view of a particular topic. Symposia may be reports of new research or reviews of established work, particularly work of an interdisciplinary nature, since the AAAS Annual Meetings typically embrace the full range of the sciences and their societal implications.

WILLIAM D. CAREY
Executive Officer
American Association for
the Advancement of Science

Contents

About the Editors and Authors x

Introduction--*Curtis C. Travis,*
Elizabeth L. Etnier 1

   References   7

1   Introduction to Groundwater Hydrology--
    Robert W. Cleary 9

   Introduction   9
   Groundwater Resources   9
   Basic Concepts of Groundwater
     Hydrology   12
     Classification of Subsurface
     Water,12; Aquifers,13; Piezometric
     Surface,15; Hydraulic Head,17;
     Hydraulic Conductivity: K,19;
     Storage Coefficient: S,21; Specific
     Yield: Sy,21
   Groundwater Movement   23
     Darcy's Law,23; Travel Times,23
   Simple Hydrogeologic Conditions   27
     Water Table Maps,27; Groundwater
     Divides,29; Vertical Stratification,
     29
   Complicated Geohydrological
     Conditions   31
   Solute Transport and Mathematical
     Modeling   35
     An Example of Flow and Transport
     Simulation,35
   Conclusion   43
   References   43

2   The History and Extent of the Groundwater
     Pollution Problem--*David E. Burmaster* 45

     Introduction   45
     Groundwater Characteristics   46
       Hydrologic Cycle,46; Uses,46;
       Protection by Soil Mantle,47
     Fundamentals of Groundwater
       Protection   48
     Sources and Prevention of
       Contamination   49
     Contamination of Drinking Water
       Wells   51
       Recent Incidents of Contamination
       by Toxic Organic Chemicals,51;
       Groundwater Conditions and
       Trends,55; Strengths and Weaknesses
       of the Data Bases,60; Coda,61
     References   61

3   The Health Risks of Toxic Organic Chemicals
     Found in Groundwater-- *Robert H. Harris* 63

     Introduction   63
     Estimating Health Risks   64
     Evidence from Occupational
       Exposures   65
     Evidence from Human Epidemiological
       Studies   69
     Evidence from Animal Studies of
       Carcinogenicity   79
     Early Warnings from Hardeman
       County   86
     Conclusions   89
     References   90

4   Protection of Groundwater Quality--
     David W. Miller 93

     Introduction   93
     Mechanisms Affecting Groundwater
       Contamination   95
       Groundwater Flow,97; Plume
       Formation and Movement,99
     Groundwater Monitoring   105
       Introduction,105; Hydrogeologic
       Investigation,108; Design and
       Installation of Monitoring Well
       Networks,109; Sampling Monitoring

Wells,115; Frequency of Sampling,
116; Summary,116
Abatement and Remedial Measures   117
Introduction,117; Containment
Techniques,118; Aquifer Restoration
by Treatment,119
Groundwater Management   120
Regional Case History,121; Local
Case Study,123
Conclusion   128
References   129

5   Groundwater Protection Strategies:
Federal, State and Local Relationships--
James T.B. Tripp 131

Introduction   131
Existing Federal Legislation   131
Clean Water Act,131; Safe Drinking
Water Act,132; Resource Conservation
and Recovery Act,132; Toxic Substances
Control Act,133; Surface Mining Control
and Reclamation Act,133; Superfund,133;
Public Nuisance Legal Actions,133
Rationale for a National Groundwater
Protection Strategy   134
Justification for Federal Involvement,
135; Federal Ambivalence,136
Cost-Benefit Considerations   137
Case Study,138
Groundwater Quality Management
Programs   138
Aquifer Classification,138; Site
Selection,139; Non-point Sources,
139
Case Studies of Land Use Control
Programs   140
Long Island,140; New Jersey Pine
Barrens,141
Framework for National Groundwater
Protection   143
Management Programs,143; Transfer
of Development Rights,144; Land
Credit Exchange Program,144; Resource
Utilization,145; Federal Legislation,
146
Conclusion   147
References   148

About the Editors and Authors

Curtis C. Travis, *an applied mathematician, is in the Office of Risk Analysis of the Health and Safety Research Division at Oak Ridge National Laboratory, Oak Ridge, Tennessee. He is interested in the development and evaluation of mathematical models to estimate human health effects of energy technologies. He has studied the health effects of a large coal liquefaction facility, hazardous chemical incineration, and the environmental transport, dosimetry, and health effects of tritium and cadmium.*

Elizabeth L. Etnier *is on the staff of the Office of Risk Analysis at Oak Ridge National Laboratory. Her research has focused on the occupational, public health, and safety aspects of non-nuclear energy technologies and on assessment of the nuclear fuel cycle, particularly the environmental transport and human metabolism of tritium.*

David E. Burmaster *is an associate at Industrial Economics, Inc. in Cambridge, Massachusetts. Formerly on the staff of the President's Council on Environmental Quality, he specializes in water quality, hazardous waste management, and risk assessment.*

Robert W. Cleary *is a professor of geoscience at the University of São Paulo and is one of the principal investigators on the largest groundwater pollution study ever funded in South America. He has published on contamination of aquifers, models of sanitary landfill leachate movement, and the transport of water and chemicals through soil.*

Robert H. Harris *is codirector of the Hazardous Waste Research Program at the Center for Energy and Environmental Studies at Princeton University. A member of the President's Council on Environmental Quality, he has done studies of the carcinogenic hazards of contaminated drinking water.*

David W. Miller, *principal at Geraghty & Miller, Inc., groundwater consultants in Syosset, New York, directs groundwater contamination investigations for industry throughout the United States and is a technical advisor on numerous water supply studies abroad. He has completed major projects for EPA including the development of the* Report to Congress on Waste Disposal Practices and Their Effects on Groundwater.

James T.B. Tripp *is counsel for the Environmental Defense Fund and director of their Eastern Water Resources and Land Use Program. He specializes in water resource and land use law and has written articles on coastal zone management, federal pollution control and water resource policy, and control of groundwater pollution problems.*

Curtis C. Travis, Elizabeth L. Etnier

Introduction

Pollution of groundwater by synthetic organic compounds is a topic of increasing national concern. Traditionally, surface water supplies have been considered to be more susceptible to contamination by organic compounds than groundwater. This is due to the inherent threat of direct discharge of industrial and agricultural chemicals into surface water. However, recent analysis of groundwater aquifers indicates that many have been contaminated by a variety of synthetic organic compounds. While the long-term health impacts of low-level exposure to synthetic organic compounds are presently unknown, their presence in groundwater must be considered a significant threat to human health.

Annual production of synthetic organic chemicals (both industrial and agricultural) in the United States quadrupled during the period 1960-1980, to 9.8×10^{10} kg (U.S. International Trade Commission as cited in Bouwer, 1982). Production of these organic chemicals results in generation of more than 3.5×10^{10} kg of hazardous chemical waste each year in the United States, with only 10% being disposed of in an environmentally safe manner (Magnuson, 1980).

Once these organic chemicals enter the environment, they frequently find their way into drinking water supplies via seepage into aquifers. In a survey of 80 water supplies located throughout the United States, Symons et al. (1975) found widespread contamination in chlorinated drinking waters by trihalomethanes, carbon tetrachloride, and 1,2-dichloroethane. In another study, samples of groundwater were collected from over 1,000 New Jersey wells (Page, 1981) chosen as a representative sample for the entire state. Water samples were analyzed for 56 toxic substances: 27 light chlorinated hydrocarbons, 20 heavy chlorinated hydrocarbons, and 9 heavy metals. All of these toxic substances were detected at some level in one or more wells. The probability of contamination of New Jersey groundwater with the more prevalent species was estimated to be: 1,1,1-trichloroethane, 78%; chloroform, 64%; carbon tetrachloride, 64%; 1,1,2-trichloroethylene, 58%; trans-dichloroethylene, 51%; BHC-beta, 50%; and 100% for the nine heavy metals, arsenic, beryllium, cadmium, copper, chromium, nickel, lead, selenium, and zinc (Page, 1981).

These reports of groundwater contamination do not represent isolated cases. For example, in January 1980, 37 public wells supplying water to more than 400,000 people in 13 cities in the San Gabriel Valley of California were closed because of trichloroethylene contamination. In 1979, a Massachusetts state commission reported that private and public wells were restricted or closed in 22 towns, and that about one-third of the communities in the state had some form of chemical contamination of their drinking water supplies. The magnitude of the problem is further highlighted by the fact that the U.S. Environmental Protection Agency (EPA) has reported "serious contamination" of drinking water wells in 34 states (CEQ, 1981).

This book presents a compilation of papers describing the groundwater resource, its extent, and its uses; discusses the issues involved in the contamination and restoration of groundwater; summarizes the associated health risks of contamination by toxic chemicals; and reviews regulatory policy regarding the federal-state strategy for the protection and preservation of this natural resource.

Groundwater movement occurs over a time scale measured in decades. Complex hydrogeologic conditions, combined with these long time scales, make it difficult to predict the extent of groundwater contamination. The first chapter of this book, by Robert W. Cleary, provides an overview of the basic concepts of groundwater hydrology, including a discussion of hydraulic head, piezometric surface, specific yield, and Darcy's Law. Cleary discusses techniques for estimation of groundwater travel times, and use of water table maps to obtain qualitative estimates of the direction and flow of groundwater movement under simple hydrogeologic conditions.

Even under simple hydrogeologic conditions it is often difficult to predict groundwater flow patterns. Such predictions may require the use of digital computer models. When aquifers are geologically complicated, sophisticated computer codes are the only means of reasonably describing groundwater movement. Such situations require extensive and expensive field work to characterize the groundwater regime. Cleary discusses some of these problems.

The insidious nature of chemical contamination of the nation's drinking water supplies is well illustrated by the chemical, aldicarb, a relatively new pesticide sold under the commercial name, Temik. It is widely distributed in the United States for application to potatoes, cotton, sugar beets, and other farm produce. Although aldicarb is highly soluble in water, and highly toxic (it is a nerve poison, fatal in high doses), it was anticipated that under normal conditions, aldicarb and its toxic residues would be entirely degraded before reaching groundwater.

Over a period of years, Temik was used by a large number of potato farmers on Long Island, but no analysis of its impact on groundwater was made until August, 1979. Nearly 8,000 private wells in potato-farming areas of Long Island were sampled (Harris and Davids, 1982). Of the 1,832 wells sampled in the town of Southhampton, 29% showed contamination by aldicarb, with 15% exceeding the New York State Department of Health (NYSDOH) guidelines of 7 parts per billion (ppb). In 1980, Temik was banned for agricultural use on Long Island. A recent study by the Cornell University Center for Environmental Research (McIntyre, 1983) estimates that Temik in Long Island's drinking water could persist at concentrations above the NYSDOH limit (7 ppb) for another 100–140 years.

In late 1982, aldicarb was detected in at least eight wells in Florida, with the highest concentration detected at 315 ppb, a factor of 30 times higher than the EPA's recommended safety threshold for drinking water (10 ppb). Consequently, the use of Temik has been banned in Florida until the end of 1983, to enable scientists to determine the extent of its presence in drinking water (Gruson, 1983). A factor contributing to concern is that the three principle potato-growing counties in Florida lie atop the Floridian Aquifer, which supplies drinking water for 42% of the state (Gruson, 1983).

In the second chapter, David E. Burmaster provides some insight into the extent of the groundwater pollution problem. During the last ten years, synthetic organic chemicals have been found in drinking water wells in virtually every state. These cases have been reported from rural, suburban, and urban areas. Although they suggest that contamination is widespread, lack of data makes a thorough analysis difficult. Burmaster presents data pertaining to levels of organic contaminants found in drinking water wells in the United States. Whether these data adequately reflect the extent of the problem is not known. Almost every case study to date has focused on known areas of groundwater contamination. However, in many areas of the country, unsuspected groundwater contamination exists due to unidentified waste disposal sites or long-term use of agricultural chemicals.

In Chapter 3, Robert Harris discusses health effects associated with groundwater pollution. Unfortunately, there is a noticeable dearth of information relating public health impacts to concentrations of chemicals in groundwater. It has been reported that the number of chemical compounds currently used in the United States exceeds 3 million, with approximately 3,000 new ones being added each year (OTA, 1983). Health effects data are only available for a small number of these chemicals, with most of the available data derived from animal studies. The difficulties and uncertainties involved in extrapolating animal data to humans are well documented. Existing data on health and environmental effects of chemicals are far from complete and many of the issues involved in the transport, fate, and environmental impacts of chemicals are poorly understood. There are virtually no data concerning interactions among chemicals during environmental transport, or concerning potential health effects of complex mixtures of chemicals.

The difficulties in linking health effects with exposures to toxic substances in drinking water are demonstrated by a case reported in Woburn, Massachusetts (Houk, 1982). In 1979, a cluster of six leukemia cases diagnosed in children living within a 6-block area was reported to the Center for Disease Control in Atlanta. An assessment of cancer mortality rates for the entire town showed statistically significant elevations of all cancers, in particular, childhood leukemia and kidney cancer. The concern regarding excess cancers focused on toxic waste disposal sites in the town. From the 1850's till the 1920's, Woburn was a major center for commercial tanning of hides and chemical production of pesticides. In the 1970's, several abandoned waste disposal sites containing hides or chemicals were discovered. Concern about possible leaching of waste chemicals led to testing of the town's drinking water wells. Two of the 11 wells showed excessive levels of organic chemicals, in particular trichloroethylene, and were located close to the neighborhood where the six leukemia cases occurred.

Epidemiological investigators obtained data attempting to correlate health effects with exposures to toxic chemicals, and found no causal factors for either leukemia or kidney cancer. The principle difficulty was that the magnitude of chemical exposure of persons having the disease in question could not be documented, and therefore no direct link could be made between excess cancer cases (in particular childhood leukemia) and exposure to specific toxic substances in drinking water (Houk, 1982).

The lack of progress in gathering and analyzing health effects data related to toxic substances in drinking water is becoming a major issue. There is critical need for a long-term, systematic, federal commitment to the collection of complete and reliable data on human exposures to, and effects of, organic chemicals in groundwater.

The most effective means to guarantee long-term availability of pristine groundwater resources is protection of aquifers from activities that degrade quality. Once contaminated, it is usually impossible to restore an aquifer to drinking water quality. In Chapter 4, David Miller reviews principles related to monitoring and restoration of groundwater resources. Miller discusses various physico-chemical properties of pollutants that make accurate monitoring of aquifer contamination difficult. These include fluid density, solubility, volatility, degradation, and adsorption. Groundwater monitoring techniques are reviewed, and a discussion given of the design and installation of monitoring well networks. Abatement and remedial measures are presented, but it is emphasized that these are rarely completely successful, and the best protection is prevention.

Activity relating to the development of groundwater protection strategies has escalated at the federal, state, and local levels. Growing public and congressional concern over contaminants entering groundwater resulted in EPA proposing a national groundwater policy (EPA, 1982) to coordinate state and federal groundwater protection programs. The policy acknowledges the concept of protecting groundwater quality according to current and projected future uses. In establishing this goal, the agency recognizes that not all groundwater has the same quality or potential use. Some groundwater is of high quality or located in areas of extreme scarcity. These resources should receive the greatest protection with the highest level of control. Other groundwater resources, because of existing contamination or geologic isolation, may provide little potential human or environmental benefit. These resources may require little or no governmental control.

The following principles guided EPA in the preparation of their proposed groundwater policy:

● State and local governments should have the lead role in developing and implementing groundwater protection initiatives. Such implementation will depend on each state's desire and ability to coordinate its own efforts.

● Upon request, and attainment of legislative requirements, EPA will delegate to the states national regulatory programs related to groundwater protection. EPA will implement nationally mandated programs where states are unwilling or unable to assume such responsibilities.

● EPA will develop specific guidelines for making federal regulatory decisions concerning groundwater quality. These guidelines will include types of groundwater to be protected, factors to be considered in limiting the extent of groundwater contamination, and the type and level of monitoring necessary to insure compliance with federal laws and regulations.

In Chapter 5, James T.B. Tripp reviews existing federal legislation dealing with groundwater protection; discusses the rationale for establishing a national groundwater protection policy; and proposes a framework for analyzing groundwater quality issues which defines appropriate federal, state, and local institutional relationships.

Tripp suggests that the first step in establishing any federal groundwater quality program is classification of groundwater quality. Aquifers may be divided into three classes: (1) those containing pristine, high quality groundwater with recharge areas that are largely unpolluted; (2) those in which some contamination has occurred, but which remain potable with reasonable treatment; and (3) those which are hydrogeologically isolated or which are contaminated to such an extent that they are unusable. After identification of aquifer quality, recharge areas should be identified and appropriate land use restrictions imposed to prevent degradation of groundwater quality. This implies that potential sites of contamination be limited to recharge areas of the third class of aquifers.

Such a national framework for classifying groundwater, identifying recharge areas, and prescribing land use controls based on recharge watershed conditions will provide for local and state groundwater protection strategies which are legally defensible from challenge. The proposed EPA national groundwater protection policy (EPA, 1982) is a step in this direction.

The public is becoming increasingly aware of the pollution of drinking water by synthetic organic chemicals. However, there is no synoptic compilation of data describing the extent of the problem. This book represents an attempt to highlight the methodological and conceptual difficulties inherent in protecting the nation's groundwater supplies. Despite the uncertainties involved, the authors provide a compilation of information pertaining to groundwater hydrology, the nature and extent of the groundwater pollution problem, and possible human health effects resulting from exposure to contaminated drinking water. The book also provides insight into the difficult legal issues involved in protecting groundwater quality.

We hope that this book will enhance public and political awareness of the groundwater pollution problem, and stress the need for a comprehensive federal and state groundwater protection program.

References

Bouwer, E. J. 1982. <u>Transformations of Trace Halogenated Organic Compounds in Biofilms</u>. Ph.D. Thesis, Stanford University.

Council on Environmental Quality. 1981. <u>Contamination of Ground Water by Toxic Organic Chemicals</u>. U.S. Government Printing Office, Washington, D.C. (January).

Gruson, K. 1983. "A Pesticide Too Good to be True?" <u>New York Times</u> (April 24, 1983).

Harris, D. and H. W. Davids. 1982. <u>Report on the Occurrence and Movement of Agricultural Chemicals in Groundwater: South Fork of Suffolk County</u>. Bureau of Water Resources, Suffolk County Department of Health Services, Long Island, N.Y.

Houk, V. H. 1982. "Determining the Impacts on Human Health Attributable to Hazardous Waste Sites." pp. 21-32 in Risk Assessment at Hazardous Waste Sites (F. A. Long and G. E. Schweitzer, eds.), <u>Amer</u>. <u>Chem</u>. <u>Soc</u>.

Magnuson, E. 1980. "The Poisoning of America." <u>Time</u>, pp. 58-69 (September 22).

McIntyre, M. 1983. "Report Sees 140-Year Temik Peril." Newsday (April 28).

Office of Technology Assessments (OTA). 1983. Technologies and Management Strategies for Hazardous Waste Control. U.S. Government Printing Office, Washington, D.C. (March).

Page, G. W. 1981. "Comparison of Groundwater and Surface Water for Patterns and Levels of Contamination by Toxic Substances." Env. Sci. Tech. 15(12): 1475-1481.

U.S. International Trade Commission. 1960-1980. Synthetic Organic Chemicals, U.S. Production and Sales. U.S. Government Printing Office, Washington, D.C.

1. Introduction to Groundwater Hydrology

Introduction

Within the last few years, pollution of groundwater by synthetic organic compounds has been recognized as an important environmental problem. It is increasingly apparent that groundwater is being contaminated by various waste disposal activities such as landfills, municipal and industrial wastewater discharges, and deep well disposal. Contamination is also occurring as a result of accidental spills, leaks, and the widespread use of pesticides and herbicides in agriculture. Groundwater movement occurs over a time scale measured in decades, with the result that hazardous compounds disposed of decades ago are just beginning to appear in water supplies. Complex hydrogeologic factors, and the long time scales involved, mean that it is difficult to predict the extent of groundwater contamination. Any attempt at such a prediction must rely on the principles of hydrologic transport in the subsurface environment. This chapter presents an overview of the basic concepts of groundwater hydrology.

Groundwater Resources

The permeable geologic strata underlying the United States provide enormous natural reservoirs for groundwater. In fact more than 86% of the fluid fresh water available in the United States is groundwater, which far exceeds all above-ground water stored in streams, rivers, reservoirs and lakes, including the Great Lakes. More than 98% of the world's fresh water supply is groundwater, again far exceeding the volume of surface waters. The percent of total water use obtained from groundwater for each state is shown in Figure 1. In the arid western states large quantities of water are used for irrigation and, as Figure 1 indicates, groundwater is a key supplier. One important fact not shown on the map of

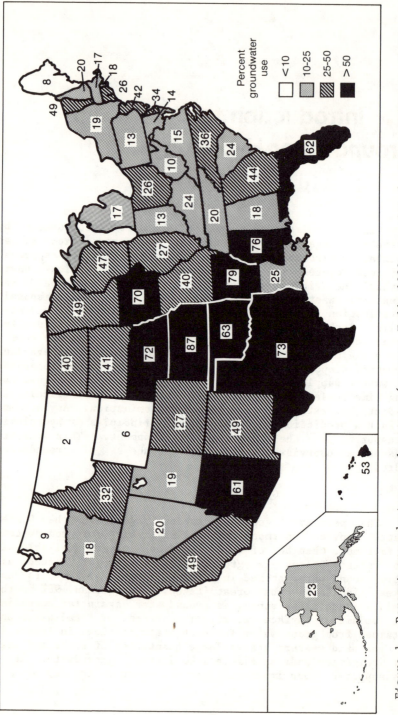

Figure 1. Percent groundwater use by state (source: Todd, 1980; reprinted with permission of John Wiley and Sons, Inc., copyright 1980).

Figure 1 is that groundwater supplies about 50% of all our drinking water and this percent is expected to increase as surface water supplies become more contaminated. (See Chapter 2 by Burmaster for a more complete discussion of groundwater use.)

Depth to groundwater may range from a few centimeters to 1000 meters or more. In the humid eastern portion of the United States depth to groundwater is rarely more than 20 meters, with an average of about 5 meters, whereas the water table in arid and semi-arid areas of the United States is often more than 50 to 100 meters below the land surface. Under natural conditions, groundwater depth depends mostly on climatic conditions. The principal source of fresh groundwater is precipitation; it is estimated for the conterminous United States that about 25% of precipitation eventually becomes groundwater (Nace, 1960).

Groundwater movement typically ranges from 1–500 meters per year. These low velocities, combined with the enormous volume of groundwater aquifers, result in detention times ranging from a few years to tens of thousands of years or more. The average age of groundwater in the United States within 800 meters of the land surface is estimated to be 200 years, while the age of groundwater greater than 800 meters from the land surface averages 10,000 years (Todd, 1980). Using carbon-14 dating techniques, Pearson and White (1967) found groundwater in a southeast Texas sandy aquifer which had fallen as precipitation 30,000 years ago. These high residence times mean that the annual renewal rate of groundwater is very small. This, together with the enormous volume of groundwater, makes it a dependable, long-term reserve effectively immune to fluctuations in precipitation. It also means that once an aquifer becomes polluted, it may be centuries or more before the system will flush itself of the contaminants.

The hydrogeological character of groundwater imparts both advantages and disadvantages to its use as a source of drinking water. The advantages of groundwater are:

● it is not subject to wide quality fluctuations.

● it is available almost everywhere. Costly transmission networks can be avoided and communities can be water independent.

● groundwater is often of high quality resulting in very low treatment costs (in many cases treatment is unnecessary or limited to disinfection only).

● with proper care, land areas above groundwater aquifers can accommodate industry, housing, farming, and recreation.

● groundwater aquifers store tremendous quantities of water without the use of dams and with negligible evaporation problems.

Disadvantages associated with the use of groundwater as drinking water are:

● deep wells can have high concentrations of mineral ions such as Ca, Mg, Mn, and Fe. Hydrogen sulfide, sulfates, and chlorides can also be present. Occasionally high concentrations of fluoride (particularly in the West) are present.

● anaerobic decomposition of buried organic matter can contaminate groundwater with such gaseous products as methane, ammonia and hydrogen sulfide.

● in the vicinity of coastal areas, salt water intrusion can occur.

● most important, once a groundwater aquifer is polluted, it is difficult, if not impossible, to clean up.

Basic Concepts of Groundwater Hydrology

Groundwater hydrology is the science that deals with the occurrence and movement of water below the earth's surface. The term groundwater usually refers to subsurface water that occurs in the fully saturated geologic strata beneath the water table. Two primary objectives of groundwater hydrology are the establishment of direction and velocity of groundwater flow. To accomplish these objectives it is necessary to understand several fundamental concepts which underlie the occurrence and movement of groundwater.

Classification of Subsurface Water

Subsurface water may be described in many ways. The traditional approach, used here, views subsurface water as occurring in two distinct zones: the vadose zone (also known as the zone of aeration) and the zone of saturation (Figure 2). The zone between the land surface and the water table is called the vadose zone. Water in this zone is under a pressure less than atmospheric with capillary forces and associated effects predominating. A well, placed in this zone, will not yield water. The vadose zone is divided into four belts, exhibiting a gradual transition from one belt to the other (Figure 2). The interstices of the first three belts of the vadose zone are occupied by water and air, except when excessive water enters the ground temporarily, e.g., during heavy rainfall. At the bottom of the vadose zone is the capillary fringe, separating the vadose and saturated zones. The capillary fringe is a curiosity in groundwater in that for uniform soils it is <u>saturated</u> but under low <u>negative</u> pressure. Thus, a well placed into this zone will not yield water due to the negative pressure which is typically of the order of -5 to -30 cm of water for coarse to medium sands and up to -200 cm of water or less for dispersed clay soils.

Any water entering the vadose zone from the land surface is affected by gravitational and capillary forces as well as evapotranspirational effects. Water movement through this zone is much slower than movement in the saturated, groundwater zone and is very difficult to describe quantitatively. Notwithstanding these complications, the vadose zone is of great interest because the majority of contaminants which pollute groundwater aquifers must pass through this zone. Because of the presence of air in this zone and relatively long residence times, many contaminants have an opportunity to biologically degrade, adsorb onto soil particles, or chemically react to form more innocuous products. Hydrobiochemical phenomena in this zone are currently the subject of active groundwater research.

Below the capillary fringe lies the zone of saturation where all the interstices are filled with water which is under a pressure greater than atmospheric pressure. Water in the zone of saturation can move freely under the influence of gravity into wells, tunnels, rivers, lakes or seas, or exit onto the land surface in the form of springs or seeps. The upper surface of the saturated, or groundwater, zone is known as the water table or phreatic surface. This surface is at atmospheric pressure and is free to rise and fall since there is no confining geologic material above it.

<u>Aquifers</u>

An aquifer is a geologic formation capable of transmitting and yielding significant quantities of water. It is estimated that over 90% of all developed aquifers consist

Zone of Aeration	Soil water is near enough to the surface to be reached by the roots of common plants. Some soil water remains after plants begin to wilt.	
	Stored or pellicular water adheres to soil particles and is not moved by gravity.	
Suspended Water	Gravity or vadose water moves downward throughout the zone.	
	Capillary water occurs only in the capillary fringe at the bottom of the zone of aeration.	
Zone of Saturation	Free water occurs below the water table. Movement controlled by the slope of the water table.	
	Confined or artesian water occurs beneath a confining stratum. A piezometric surface results.	
Groundwater	Fixed groundwater occurs in sub-capillary openings of clays, silts, etc. It is not affected by gravity.	
	Connate water entrapped in rocks at the time of their deposition.	

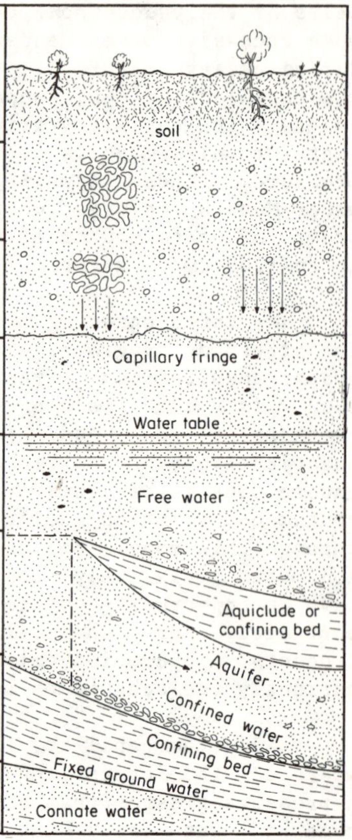

Figure 2. Occurrences of water in geologic formations.

of unconsolidated sands and gravels found in coastal plains, alluvial valleys, and glacial deposits. Sandstones, porous basalts, and limestones with developed solution channels may also make suitable aquifers. In some areas of the United States, fractured hard rock, such as granite, has been drilled to supply water, but the yields are quite low compared to aquifers of sand and gravel. From a geometric viewpoint, most aquifers have a very large areal extent in comparison to their vertical thickness (on the order of kilometers vs. meters).

Aquifers are classified as confined or unconfined depending upon the absence or presence of a water table. An unconfined aquifer is one in which the water table acts as the upper surface of the zone of saturation. Bouwer (1978) has described them as underground lakes in porous materials. Confined aquifers are usually under pressures much greater than atmospheric, and are bounded above and below by impervious or semi-pervious strata. Figure 3 illustrates various types of aquifers and aquifer characteristics. Aquifer A is an unconfined aquifer with a water table, the surface of which is at atmospheric pressure. The characterizations above the figure refer to aquifer B which is the middle aquifer between aquifer A (a water table or unconfined aquifer) and aquifer C (a confined aquifer like aquifer B).

Piezometric Surface

Water levels in wells penetrating an unconfined aquifer, undergoing horizontal flow, will be equal to the level of the adjacent water table, which also serves as the upper physical boundary of the aquifer (see aquifer A, Figure 3). On the other hand, water in wells penetrating a confined aquifer will generally rise above the base of the upper confining formation to levels determined by the pressure distribution within the aquifer (see aquifers B and C in Figure 3). When these equilibrium water levels are connected, a surface will be formed which is called the piezometric surface. This surface, unlike the water table surface, does not serve as the upper physical boundary of the aquifer. In fact, the piezometric surface is an imaginary surface determined by the pressure distribution within the aquifer. It takes on physical meaning only when the aquifer is punctured by wells, and the water rises up each well commensurate with the pressure at that location. Thus, the piezometric surface is an imaginary surface defining the level that water would rise to in any well puncturing the aquifer.

The upper physical boundary of confined aquifers is the upper confining layer itself. The piezometric surface may lie

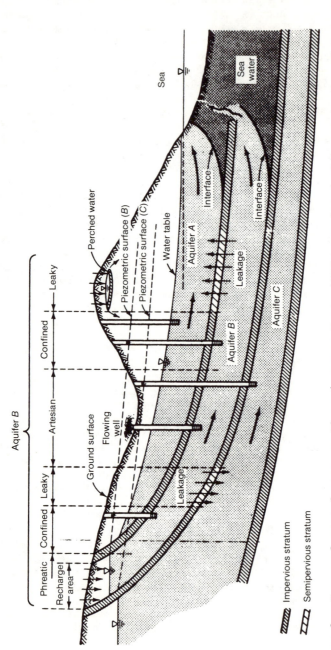

Figure 3. Types of groundwater aquifers (source: Bear, 1979; reprinted with permission of McGraw-Hill Book Company; copyright 1979).

anywhere from the upper confining layer to above the land
surface itself. When it lies above the land surface, a well
puncturing the aquifer at that point will see the water rise
up from the aquifer seeking its above-ground piezometric
surface. If the top of the well itself is below the
piezometric surface, water will simply flow out onto the
ground resulting in what is called a flowing well.

Aquifer B in Figure 3 illustrates many of these concepts.
As we move from left to right across the figure, aquifer B
changes in status. In the upper left-hand corner of the
figure, we see that aquifer B outcrops to the land surface
allowing direct recharge to take place through a free surface.
Since the surface is free, aquifer B in that region is, in
fact, phreatic, or unconfined (a water table aquifer). The
piezometric surface of aquifer B is described by the upper
dotted line extending from the recharge area towards the right
of the figure. This sloping dotted line indicates the water
level that would be reached in any well puncturing aquifer B.
For example, in the middle of the figure, the piezometric
surface is above the land surface and since the top of the
well is below this surface, water flows out onto the ground as
it seeks to reach its piezometric surface. Aquifer B is
confined by semi-pervious strata in two locations allowing
water to leak out of or in to the aquifer. The direction and
rate of leakage is determined by the relative difference in
height of the piezometric surfaces or water table surface (in
the case of aquifer A) of the two adjoining aquifers.

When semi-pervious or impervious material of limited
areal extent is located between the land surface and the
principal water table aquifer below, a small, perched, water
table may form (see the upper right half of Figure 3). Such a
perched water table has limited capacity and should not be
confused with the true location of the main water table during
a drilling program.

Hydraulic Head

The hydraulic head is defined as the vertical distance
from a reference datum (typically mean sea level) to the
piezometric surface or water table surface. Groundwater
always moves from higher hydraulic head locations towards
lower hydraulic head locations. It may move "uphill",
topographically speaking, but it must always move "downhill",
hydraulically speaking. Hydraulic head is also called
piezometric head or total potential. On the right half of the
figure one can see that the piezometric surface of B is higher
than the piezometric surface of C, and the location of the top

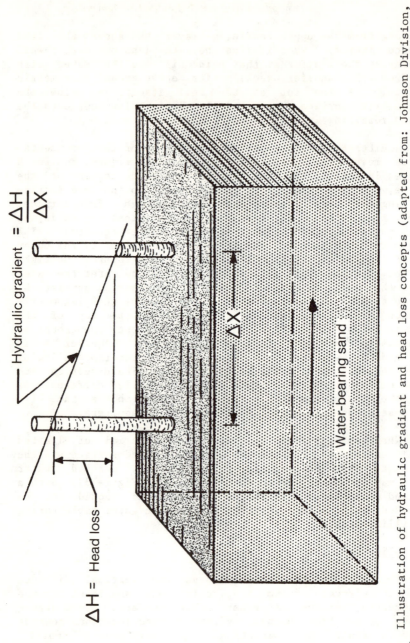

Figure 4. Illustration of hydraulic gradient and head loss concepts (adapted from: Johnson Division, UOP, 1982).

of the water table of aquifer A. Thus, water in aquifer B, in
the semi-pervious areas, will move into aquifer A or C. The
driving force influencing the movement is the piezometric head
difference.

In simple terms, hydraulic head is a measure of the total
energy of the water at a given location, which is the sum of
its kinetic energy, pressure energy, and elevation energy.
Since groundwater moves very slowly, the kinetic energy
contribution may be neglected and the hydraulic head is then
simply the sum of a pressure head and an elevation head. As
groundwater moves from one point to another, friction must be
overcome, resulting in a decrease in the hydraulic head, or a
head loss over the distance traveled. Figure 4 illustrates
the head loss between two locations and notes that this loss
divided by the distance between the points is called the
hydraulic gradient. The hydraulic gradient is always
negative, since water always flows in the direction of
decreasing hydraulic head. We will see later, when Darcy's
Law is discussed, that the rate of groundwater flow is
directly proportional to the hydraulic gradient.

While an understanding of the theory behind the term
hydraulic head may require some background in fluid mechanics,
in practice it is quite easy to measure and to apply. As
mentioned earlier, the hydraulic head is the sum of the
pressure head and the elevation head, or simply the vertical
distance from a stated datum plane to the water level in the
well. Since it is usually impossible to measure this distance
directly, it is done indirectly as Figure 5 illustrates. One
measures the depth to water from the top of the well casing
(this can be done with an electric tape or a steel surveyor's
tape and chalk) and subtracts this reading from the height of
the well casing above a given datum (this measurement is
carefully performed with accurate surveying equipment and
reference surveyor's marks). This difference is termed the
hydraulic head relative to the stated datum.

Hydraulic Conductivity: K

Hydraulic conductivity is a measure of an aquifer's
ability to conduct water under the influence of a hydraulic
gradient. It is defined as the volume of water that will move
through a unit area in unit time. Thus, hydraulic
conductivity has units of velocity (L/T). It is a property of
both the porous medium and the fluid flowing through it. The
higher the conductivity, the better the aquifer conducts
water. For example, clean sands may have conductivities

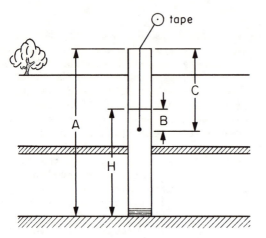

A = top of casing elev. above datum

B = length of wetted tape

C = tape reading, read exactly at the top of the casing

H = piezometric head, relative to a given datum

DATUM

C – B = DTW = depth to water

A – DTW = H = piezometric head at the center of the screen, relative to the indicated datum plane

Figure 5. Field measurement of hydraulic head.

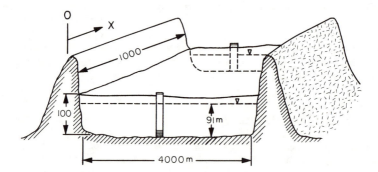

Figure 6. Application of Darcy's Law in a bedrock valley.

ranging from 0.1 to 0.001 cm/sec, while unweathered clay may have conductivities ranging from 1 x 10^{-7} to 1 x 10^{-9} cm/sec.

Storage Coefficient: S

The storage coefficient is defined as the volume of water an aquifer releases from or takes into storage per unit surface area of aquifer per unit change in the hydraulic head normal to that surface. The storage coefficient is a dimensionless quantity expressing the volume of water released per volume of aquifer. Practically speaking, for a 1 meter by 1 meter vertical column extending through an aquifer, the storage coefficient equals the volume of water (in cubic meters) released from the aquifer when the piezometric head declines 1 meter. In most confined aquifers, S ranges from 5 x 10^{-3} to 5 x 10^{-5}, indicating that large pressure changes over extensive areas are required to produce substantial yields in confined aquifers.

Specific Yield: S_y

Specific yield, S_y, is defined as the volume of water that a saturated soil will yield per unit volume of aquifer under the sole influence of gravity. That is, S_y represents the ratio of the volume of water released from the aquifer (under the influence of gravity) to the total volume of the aquifer. S_y for an unconfined aquifer is essentially equal to its storage coefficient. Most unconfined sandy aquifers have specific yields in the range of 0.10 to 0.30. Water recharged to or discharged from a water table aquifer represents a direct change in the storage volume of the aquifer. This change in volume may be calculated by multiplying the specific yield by the change in volume of the aquifer over a period of time. For example, if a water table aquifer with a specific yield of 0.25, and measuring 1000 meters by 1000 meters in areal extent, declines 4 meters due to pumping, the amount of water released is: 0.25 x 1000 x 1000 x 4 = 1 x 10^6 cubic meters. The converse is also interesting: if the contents of a surface lagoon containing 1 x 10^6 cubic meters of water and measuring 1000 meters by 1000 meters by 1 meter deep were to reach the groundwater, the water table would rise 4 meters and not 1 meter. This illustrates the effect of porosity on the storage of groundwater. Specific yield is also known as effective or drainable porosity (n_e). See Table 1 for typical values of effective porosity. In pollutant transport calculations one uses the effective porosity for flow through the medium (n_{ef}). In most cases, n_{ef} is assumed to be n_e, but it may be less than n_e if the aquifer has appreciable immobile water (dead zones).

Table 1. Typical values of effective porosity (or specific
          yield) of aquifer materials (from McWhorter and
          Sunada, 1977)

Aquifer material	Range	Arithmetic mean
Sedimentary materials		
Sandstone (fine)	0.02-0.40	0.21
Sandstone (medium)	0.12-0.41	0.27
Siltstone	0.01-0.33	0.12
Sand (fine)	0.01-0.46	0.33
Sand (medium)	0.16-0.46	0.32
Sand (coarse)	0.18-0.43	0.30
Gravel (fine)	0.13-0.40	0.28
Gravel (medium)	0.17-0.44	0.24
Gravel (coarse)	0.13-0.25	0.21
Silt	0.01-0.39	0.20
Clay	0.01-0.18	0.06
Limestone	~0-0.36	0.14
Wind-Laid Materials		
Loess	0.14-0.22	0.18
Eolian Sand	0.32-0.47	0.38
Tuff	0.02-0.47	0.21
Metamorphic Rock		
Schist	0.22-0.33	0.26

Groundwater Movement

Darcy's Law
_____

In 1856, a French engineer named Henri Darcy published results on the flow of water through sand filter beds. This experimental work resulted in the establishment of the basic law of groundwater movement, termed Darcy's Law. Darcy concluded that the rate of flow of water through sand beds is directly proportional to the head loss over the bed, and inversely proportional to the thickness of the bed. Mathematically, his findings can be stated in the following way:

$$q = Q / A = - K \frac{\Delta H}{\Delta X}$$

where q is the Darcy velocity (L/T), Q is the flow rate (L^3T), A is the cross-sectional area perpendicular to the flow direction (L^2), K is the hydraulic conductivity (L/T) and ΔH is the hydraulic head loss (L) over the distance ΔX (L).

As a simple application of Darcy's Law, consider the valley illustrated in Figure 6. It is of uniform cross-sectional area with impermeable surfaces on the bottom and both sides, containing groundwater flowing through coarse sand. The hydraulic head decreases 1 meter for every 1000 meters of length along the valley. The hydraulic conductivity is 300 meters/day and the average height and width of the saturated aquifer is 91 and 4000 meters, respectively. Assuming horizontal flow and no additions or withdrawals to or from the aquifer, we may estimate the volume rate of flow of groundwater through the valley using Darcy's Law:

$$Q = - K A \frac{\Delta H}{\Delta X}$$

$$Q = - (300) (91) (4000) (-1/1000)$$

$$Q = 109,200 \ m^3/day$$

Travel Times
_____

In many groundwater quality problems, it is of interest to estimate how long it will take a pollutant to travel from one location to another. This travel time may be estimated by collecting hydrological data for the aquifer in question and applying Darcy's Law. Figure 7 shows a sanitary landfill located 16,000 feet from a river. The aquifer is unconfined with a hydraulic conductivity of 900 feet/day and an effective flow porosity (n_{ef}) of 0.25. A number of observation wells

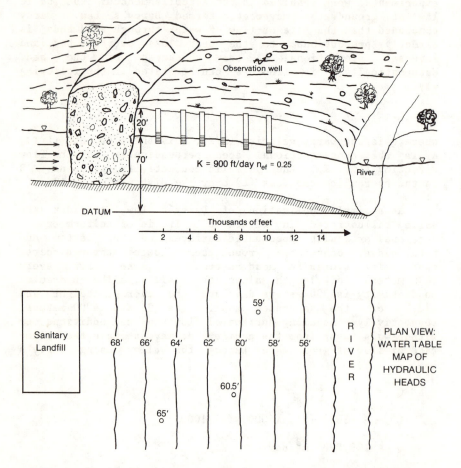

Figure 7. Application of Darcy's Law to estimate time of pollutant travel in aquifers.

have been drilled and the depth to groundwater from the tops
of the well casings have been measured. The tops of the well
casings have been surveyed and their elevations above the
indicated datum are known. The hydraulic head at each
observation well is found by subtracting the depth to
groundwater from the casing elevation. The lower half of the
figure illustrates a water table map which was constructed by
connecting points of equal hydraulic head. These lines of
equal hydraulic head are called equipotential lines and for
isotropic geologic materials, the direction of groundwater
movement will always be perpendicular to the lines of equal
potential (when drawn on such a map these lines are called
flow lines or streamlines). In this example, the
equipotential lines are all parallel to the river and so the
groundwater will flow through the sanitary landfill directly
to the river. To estimate the velocity of flow, one selects
any two equipotential lines and applies Darcy's Law. For
example, the hydraulic head loss between 4000 and 6000 feet is
2 feet (66 feet – 64 feet). The Darcy velocity in this
aquifer is therefore:

$$q = -K \frac{\Delta H}{\Delta X} = -(900)(64-66/6000-4000)$$

$$q = 0.9 \text{ feet/day}$$

The Darcy velocity is based on the entire cross-sectional area
which includes voids and soil grains. Since groundwater can
only move through void spaces, the true velocity (also known
as the real or seepage velocity) is calculated by dividing the
Darcy velocity by the effective flow porosity [n_{ef}(Bear,
1979)].

$$V_s = \text{seepage velocity} = \frac{\text{Darcy Velocity}}{\text{effective flow porosity}}$$

$$V_s = \frac{0.9 \text{ ft/day}}{0.25} = 3.6 \text{ feet/day}$$

The travel time can now be calculated by dividing this true
velocity into the distance of interest. The travel time for
an average particle of contaminated water to reach the river,
for example, would be:

$$T = 16,000/3.6 = 12.2 \text{ years}$$

In this example, the average velocity of a particle of
contaminated groundwater was estimated to be 3.6 feet/day. In
reality, some contaminated water is moving faster than this
velocity, and some waters are moving slower due to dispersive
and/or adsorptive phenomena in the geologic material.
Generally these dispersive phenomena tend to dilute the

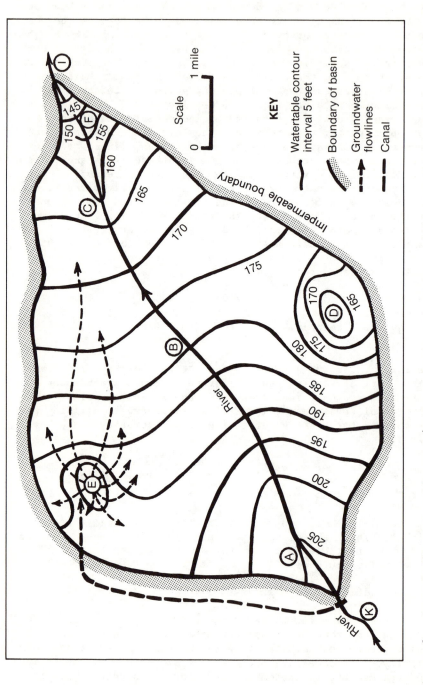

KEY

Watertable contour interval 5 feet

Boundary of basin

Groundwater flowlines

Canal

Scale

0   1 mile

Figure 8. A typical water table map (source: Davis and DeWiest, 1966; reprinted with permission from John Wiley and Sons, Inc., copyright 1966).

contaminant concentration so that early arriving particles of contaminated water are much less concentrated than can be found at the source. Adsorptive phenomena, when significant, cause contaminants to effectively move slower than the uncontaminated groundwater.

In sedimentary deposits, it is not uncommon to find vertical stratification of hydraulic conductivity. A particularly "fast" layer of soil (one with a higher hydraulic conductivity) might be sandwiched between two slower layers. This would allow groundwater to pass more quickly than one would estimate using an average, lower hydraulic conductivity. Because of potential vertical stratification problems, it is advisable to confirm their presence or absence with multiple-level field data before making conclusions based on the assumption of uniform flow throughout the vertical cross-section. In practice, to be on the safe side, one includes a safety factor when estimating travel time.

Simple Hydrogeologic Conditions

Many shallow aquifers are governed by uniform horizontal flow conditions and uncomplicated geology. Fortunately for practicing hydrologists, in these situations, an easily constructed water table map is sufficient to estimate the direction and rate of groundwater movement. In constructing such a map, it is assumed that the aquifer is isotropic, homogeneous, and characterized by two-dimensional flow (usually in the areal plane). Many aquifers satisfy these conditions. A water table map is constructed by connecting points of equal hydraulic head (lines of equal potential). Flow lines are then drawn perpendicular to the equipotential lines, delineating directions of groundwater flow. The map also indicates recharge areas, pumping centers, groundwater divides, and where rivers are effluent (groundwater flows from the aquifer into the river) or influent (river water flows into the aquifer).

Water Table Maps

A water table map constructed from hydraulic head data is illustrated in Figure 8. One can see by making a section cut at point A that as one moves away from the river the hydraulic head decreases progressively. Since at point A the head is higher at the river than in the surrounding aquifer, water flows from the river into the aquifer, and the river is termed influent. At point C, the opposite is true; the heads in the surrounding aquifer are higher than at the river, and therefore water will flow from the aquifer into the river. The river is termed effluent under such conditions. At point

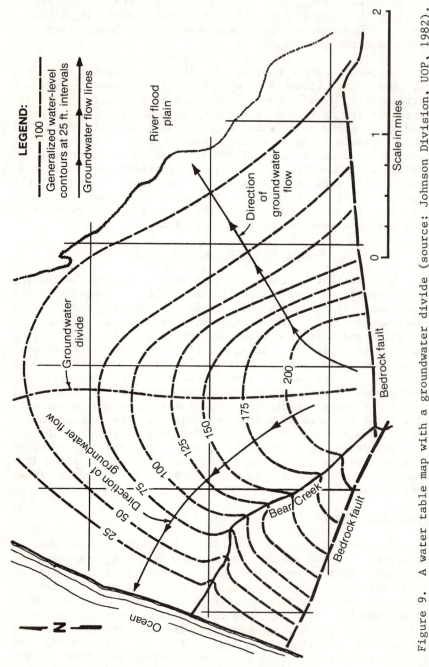

LEGEND:

—— 100 —— Generalized water-level
contours at 25 ft. intervals

→ Groundwater flow lines

River flood
plain

Direction
of
groundwater
flow

Groundwater
divide

Direction of
groundwater flow

200

175

150

125

100

75

50

25

Bedrock fault

Bear Creek

Bedrock fault

Ocean

N

Scale in miles

0   1   2

Figure 9.   A water table map with a groundwater divide (source: Johnson Division, UOP, 1982).

B, the hydraulic head in the aquifer is equal to the head in the river and the river is neither influent nor effluent. At point D one can see a cone of depression indicating operation of a pumping well which causes a groundwater drawdown. Point E depicts a mounding situation where water has been diverted from the river at point K and spread on the land at point E. Eventually this water will enter the river again as indicated by the dotted flow lines (perpendicular to lines of equal potential). These infiltration operations are common in Europe where the natural filtering and purification properties of aquifers are utilized.

Groundwater Divides

A water table map illustrating the effects of a groundwater divide is given in Figure 9. The dotted lines represent lines of equal potential and the solid lines represent flow lines. Water entering the aquifer from the right of the figure will eventually flow to the river flood plain, while water entering from the left of the groundwater divide will flow to the ocean. If these contours remain constant, one could say that the construction of a sanitary landfill on the right-half of the figure would not threaten Bear Creek. However, there can be seasonal variation in hydraulic head causing inaccuracies in conclusions based on groundwater data collected during only one season of the year.

Vertical Stratification

Water table maps, almost by definition, characterize groundwater flow in an areal plane. The same principles, however, hold for vertical flow as long as there is no significant hydraulic head variation in the remaining dimension, or significant vertical stratification of soil properties. In situations where vertical stratification does not appear to be significant, a simple water table map can be constructed. An example is given in Figure 10, which represents Perch Lake in Chalk River, Ontario, Canada (Killey, 1977). The hydraulic head data for this site was collected from multiple piezometers. The solid lines are lines of equal hydraulic head and the dotted line is a flow line indicating upward flow into the lake. The rate and direction of groundwater movement constructed from water table maps such as this (containing vertical cross-sections) must be considered rough estimates. In such cases, there are likely to be significant differences between horizontal and vertical hydraulic conductivity . Such differences render the aquifer anisotropic, and flow lines are no longer perpendicular to lines of equal potential. Water table maps for these

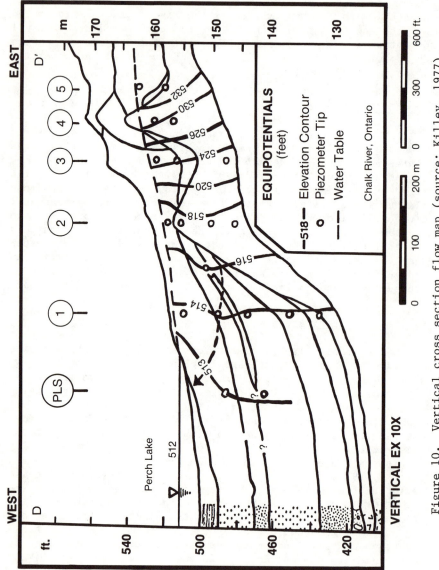

Figure 10. Vertical cross section flow map (source: Killey, 1977).

situations, however, can still be constructed using variable transformations (Freeze and Cherry, 1979).

Complicated Geohydrological Conditions

Many aquifers are geologically complicated due to heterogeneous soil properties, layering, or unusual boundary or internal conditions. For such aquifers, and for multiple-aquifer situations, the mathematics of groundwater movement is relatively sophisticated, involving the unsteady-state solution of partial differential equations. These equations are solved analytically or numerically with the use of a digital computer. Their solutions allow prediction of the rate and direction of groundwater movement under a variety of conditions. For geologically complicated aquifers, these equations and accompanying sophisticated computer codes are the only means to reasonably describe the associated groundwater movement. Application of these codes requires a detailed three-dimensional description of the hydrogeologic properties of the aquifer. Acquisition of these parameters may be costly and time-consuming.

Figure 11 illustrates the effect of a highly permeable lens (black in figure 11) in an otherwise uniform aquifer. The lens causes distortion of the flow lines with water converging into the lens on the left side and diverging from the lens on the right side. To predict such flow patterns one would almost certainly have to use a digital computer model. Figure 12 also illustrates the effects of three highly permeable lenses (stipled areas) in an otherwise uniform aquifer. The upper right-hand corner of the figure shows four possible locations (W, X, Y and Z) for a hazardous waste landfill or industrial lagoon. Following the solid water flow lines from each of these locations, extremely different flow paths and detention times in the aquifer are apparent. The complexity of flow through this groundwater basin is caused by impressed boundary conditions and the three highly permeable lenses. Once again, a simple water table map would have been wholly inappropriate to estimate the rates and directions of groundwater flow. In fact, Freeze (1972) used a two-dimensional digital computer flow model to characterize this aquifer.

In certain parts of the United States high-yielding aquifers such as unconsolidated sands and gravels do not exist. Instead, these areas may rely on aquifers consisting of fractured hard rock for their water supply. Yields from such aquifers are not high, but for individual homes or small municipal demands, they can be appropriate. As Figure 13 illustrates, fractured rock aquifers are an excellent example of groundwater flow under complicated geohydrological

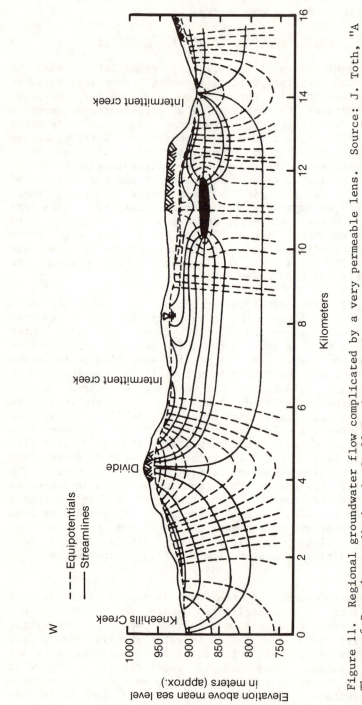

Figure 11. Regional groundwater flow complicated by a very permeable lens. Source: J. Toth, "A Theory of Groundwater Motion in Small Drainage Basins in Central Alberta, Canada." Journal of Geophysical Research 67, no. 11 (1962), p. 4375.

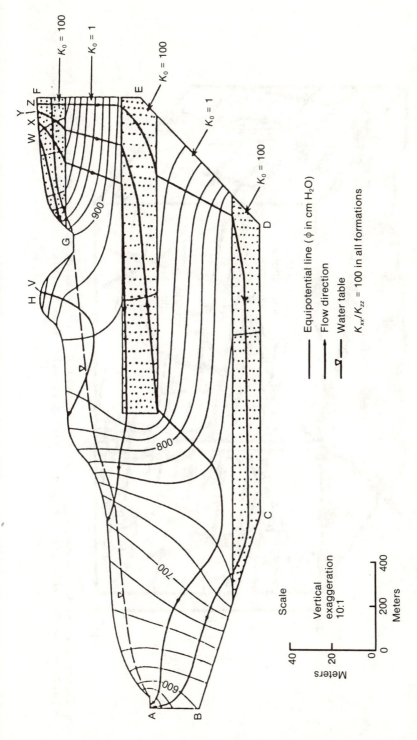

Figure 12. Influence of permeable lenses on regional flow in a vertical cross section (source: Freeze, 1972; copyright 1972 by International Business Machines Corporation; with permission).

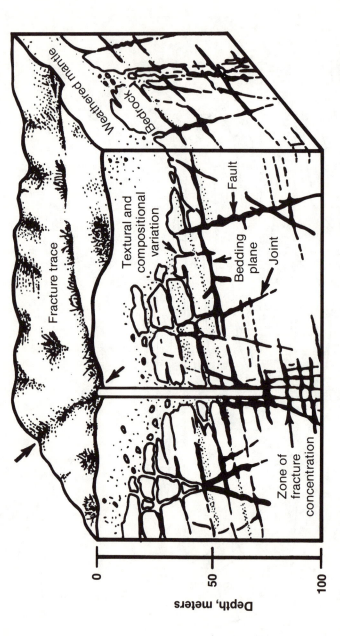

Figure 13. Illustration of geologic complications on groundwater flow in fractured rock (source: Lattman and Parizek, 1964; reprinted with permission from Elsevier Scientific Publishing Co.).

conditions. A simple analysis is generally inappropriate for such cases and many examples exist where even the use of sophisticated digital computer models is inadequate to predict the rate and direction of groundwater movement. Such situations often require extensive and expensive field work to characterize the groundwater regime.

Solute Transport and Mathematical Modeling

This chapter provides an overview of the basic concepts of groundwater hydrology as they relate to rate and direction of groundwater flow. In general, a complete characterization of contamination leaching from a waste disposal site involves not only the description of groundwater movement (known as the flow problem) but also a description of the movement of individual chemicals dissolved in the groundwater (known as the transport problem). The complete analysis involves a semi-coupled, two-step procedure with the solution of the flow problem (directions and velocities) serving as input to the transport problem. The final result gives concentrations of individual chemical species as a function of space and time under given initial, boundary, and physico-chemical conditions. With few exceptions, solute transport analysis is almost always done with the use of a computer model.

The transport problem, complicated by the chemical processes and reactions operating in the soil-water system as well as hydrogeologic dispersion phenomena is an order of magnitude more difficult to solve than the flow problem. These physico-chemical processes include adsorption, desorption, precipitation, dissolution, ion exchange, biochemical reactions, and chemical transformations. Some of these processes have the net effect of causing chemical species to move at lower velocities than the groundwater. The demands on computer memory and time can be enormous or even prohibitive since each chemical species must be described by its own partial differential transport equation as well as chemical equilibria relationships which describe its interactions with other chemicals. For this reason almost all multi-dimensional modeling studies to date have involved only one species. Multi-species modeling involving more than three species is under active research but it is several years away from practical application at hazardous waste sites.

An Example of Flow and Transport Simulation

Toxic waste contamination is currently threatening the public water supply wells of Atlantic City, New Jersey. Millions of gallons of hazardous liquid wastes were dumped over many years in an abandoned sand and gravel quarry known

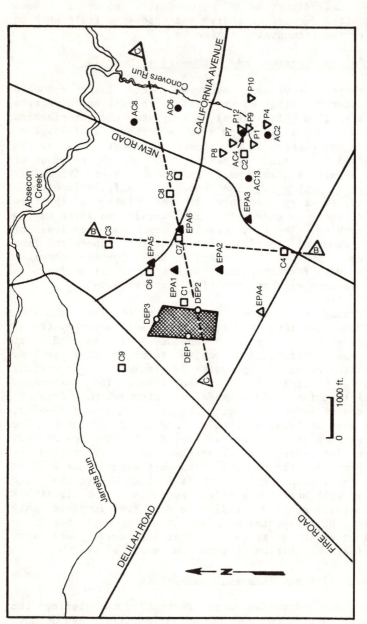

Figure 14. Vicinity of Price Landfill (shaded region) with survey wells screened in upper zone of the Cohansey aquifer indicated. The Atlantic City (AC) wells to the east are the municipal water supply wells that are threatened by the contamination. Other wells in the figure are: New Jersey Department of Environmental Protection (DEP), U.S. Environmental Protection Agency (EPA), and a C and P series of wells installed by a consulting firm to allow for detection of hydrologic parameters.

as Prince's Landfill. The landfill is located above the Cohansey aquifer, about 1000 meters west and upgradient of the nearest municipal supply well, as illustrated in Figure 14. Due to the urgency of the problem, the site was ranked in the top 10 of the first 115 top-priority Superfund clean-up sites chosen by the United States Environmental Protection Agency.

Working with a limited water quality data base and little information on recharge rates, boundary conditions, historical pumping rates, and head data, Gray and Hoffman (1983) presented a two-dimensional finite element modeling study of flow and transport in the vicinity of the landfill and municipal pumping wells. Figure 15 illustrates their simulation of the flow problem in the water table aquifer at the site using average municipal pumping rates for the last 10 years. The figure illustrates the dominating influence of municipal supply well AC 13 on the flow of contaminants from the dumping ground. Using the head distribution of Figure 15, the contaminant distribution of a single non-reactive species after 10 years of normal municipal pumping is illustrated in Figure 16. Since historical concentration data were not available in the landfill, the authors arbitrarily assigned a value of 100 units for concentration along the eastern border of the landfill and kept this value constant during the 10-year simulation. The contouring interval is 5 units, with the outermost contour representing 5 percent of the 100-unit concentration along the entire landfill border.

The authors investigated two remedial aquifer clean-up schemes (RS1 and RS2) involving pumping and injection to illustrate how models may be used to quickly and inexpensively investigate a range of available hydrologic alternatives. Figure 17 shows the water table contour results for the RS2 scheme where contaminated water is pumped at a rate of 10 million gallons per month (mgm) from each of 3 wells near the landfill (labelled "P" on the figure) and injected at a rate of 2 mgm into each of 4 wells east of the landfill (labelled "I"). This scheme helps to speed up the clean-up by flushing the pollutants from the system via favorable hydraulic gradients resulting from the pumping and reinjection. Figures 18 and 19 illustrate the concentration distributions which should result from utilization of such a scheme after 5 and 25 years of pumping, respectively. A comparison of the initial concentration distribution (Figure 16) with the projected concentrations after 5 and 25 years of pumping (Figures 18 and 19) shows a decrease in size of the contaminated zone and a reduction in the maximum concentration. For the hypothetical conditions simulated it is obvious that this remedial scheme must be operated many years to achieve satisfactory results.

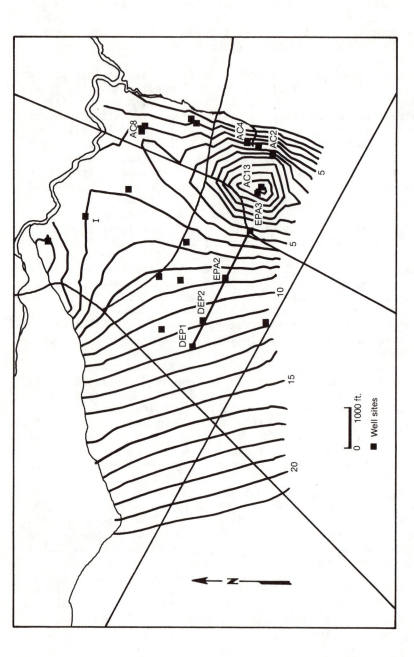

Figure 15. Simulation of water table in the upper Cohansey using pumping rates of last ten years at Atlantic City municipal wells AC2, AC4, AC8, and AC13. (■) represent various well sites. (After Gray and Hoffman, 1983).

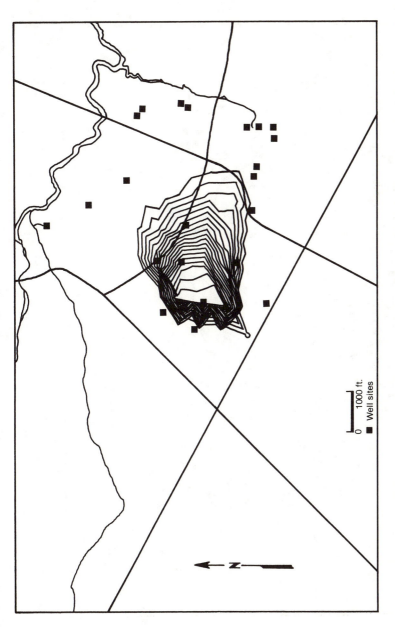

Figure 16. Contaminant distribution after ten years using the head distribution of Figure 15 (after Gray and Hoffman, 1983). The concentration at the landfill border is assumed to be 100 units, with the 20 contour intervals shown on the figure representing 5-unit increments. The outermost contour represent 5% of the original 100-unit concentration.

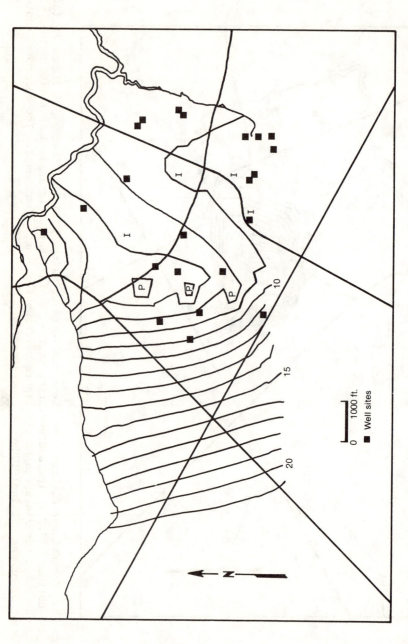

Figure 17. Water table contours for RS2 pumping 10 mgm from each well at "P" and injecting 2 mgm into each well at "I" (after Gray and Hoffman, 1983).

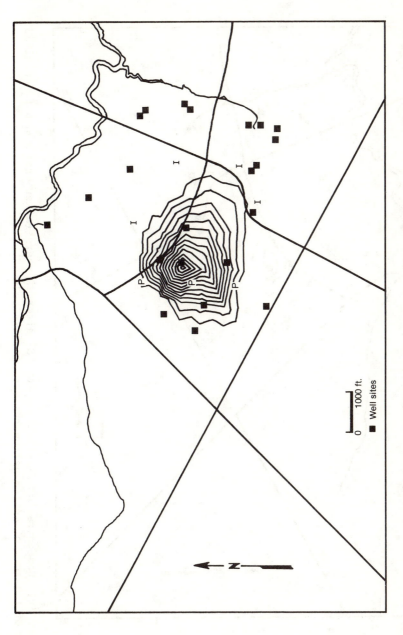

Figure 18. Concentration distribution for RS2 after 5 years (after Gray and Hoffman, 1983). During the first 5 years of pumping, the leading edge contour of the plume remains virtually stationary, but the magnitude of the highest concentration is reduced significantly.

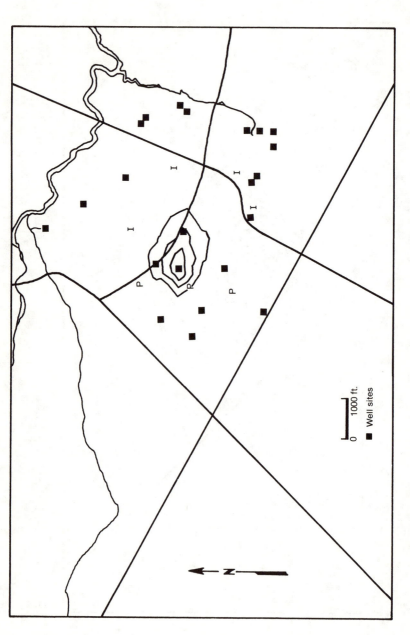

Figure 19. Concentration distribution for TS2 after 25 years (after Gray and Hoffman, 1983). The size of the zone of contamination has been greatly reduced.

Conclusion

The science of groundwater hydrology deals with the occurrence and movement of water below the earth's surface. Its primary objectives are the establishment of direction and velocity of groundwater flow, otherwise known as the flow problem. Groundwater flow is highly dependent on geologic and hydrologic conditions in the aquifer. Fortunately, many cases of interest lend themselves to simple analysis as illustrated in the water table maps of Figures 8 and 9. However, as Figures 11, 12, and 13 illustrate, there are just as many cases, if not more, requiring highly skilled hydrologists using digital computer models to determine groundwater flow patterns.

Every study of a groundwater aquifer should begin with a careful field program to define its hydrogeologic structure. With the objectives of the groundwater study defined, and adequate hydrogeologic data, one can choose an appropriate predictive approach; this can range from simple water table maps to unsteady-state, three-dimensional computer models. In general, a complete characterization of contamination leaching from a waste disposal site involves the description of groundwater movement as well as the movements of all species of materials dissolved in the groundwater. Prediction of the movement of chemicals in groundwater is known as the transport problem. It is complicated by chemical reactions operating in the soil-water system, as well as hydrologic dispersion phenomena, and is an order of magnitude more difficult to solve than the flow problem. Characterization of the concurrent transport of dissolved chemical species with groundwater necessitates the simultaneous solution of groundwater flow equations with transport equations describing chemical processes and reactions operating in the soil-water system. The description and solution of these equations are not completely developed, and represent the challenge of the 80's for groundwater scientists.

References

Bear, J. 1979. <u>Hydraulics of Groundwater</u>. McGraw-Hill International Book Co.

Bouwer, H. 1978. <u>Groundwater Hydrology</u>. McGraw-Hill International Book Co.

Davis, S. N. and R. J. M. DeWiest. 1966. <u>Hydrogeology</u>. John Wiley and Sons, Inc., New York.

Freeze, R. A. 1972. ˝Subsurface Hydrology at Waste Disposal Sites.˝ IBM Journ. Res. Develop. 16(2):117.

Freeze, R. A. and J. A. Cherry. 1979. Groundwater. Prentice-Hall, New Jersey.

Gray, W. G. and J. L. Hoffman. 1983a. ˝A Numerical Model Study of Ground-water Contamination from Price's Landfill, New Jersey - I. Data Base and Flow Simulation.˝ Groundwater 21(1):7-14.

Gray, W. G. and J. L. Hoffman. 1983b. ˝A Numerical Model Study of Ground-water Contamination from Price's Landfill, New Jersey - II. Sensitivity Analysis and Contaminant Plume Simulation.˝ Groundwater 21(1):15-21.

Johnson Division, Universal Oil Products. 1982. ˝Ground Water and Wells,˝ Johnson Div. U.O.P. Inc., St. Paul, Minnesota.

Killey, R.W.D. 1977. M.S. Thesis, Department of Earth Sciences, University of Waterloo, Waterloo, Ontario.

Lattman, L. H. and R. R. Parizek. 1964. ˝Relationship Between Fracture Traces and the Occurrence of Ground Water in Carbonate Rocks.˝ J. Hydrol. 2:73-91.

McWhorter, D. B. and D. K. Sunada. 1977. Ground-water Hydrology and Hydraulics. Water Resources Publications, P. O. Box 303, Fort Collins, CO.

Nace, R. Water Management, Agriculture and Groundwater Supplies. U.S Geological Survey Circular 415, Washington, D.C. 12 pp.

Pearson, F. J. Jr. and D. E. White. 1967. ˝Carbon 14 Ages and Flow Rates of Water in Carrizo Sand,˝ Atascosa County, Texas. Water Resources Research 3:251-261.

Todd, D. K. 1980. Groundwater Hydrology. John Wiley and Sons, New York.

Toth, J. 1962. ˝A Theory of Groundwater Motion in Small Drainage Basins in Central Alberta, Canada.˝ J. Geophysic. Res. 67(11): 4375.

David E. Burmaster

2. The History and Extent of the Groundwater Pollution Problem

Introduction

Ground water is an important economic resource. Approximately 25% of all fresh water used in the United States comes from ground water sources. Approximately 50% of all people who reside in the United States rely on ground water as their source of drinking water. These figures may surprise some people who grew up on the east and west coasts where cities such as Boston, New York, Philadelphia, Washington, D.C., Los Angeles, and San Francisco rely heavily on surface water. However, some major cities such as Miami and Tuscon, rely heavily on ground water, and the vast majority of rural residents rely exclusively on ground water.

In spite of the importance of ground water as a national resource, very little is being done to prevent its contamination by organic chemicals. Many ground water supplies of drinking water are now closed due to unacceptably high concentrations of toxic organic chemicals. Contamination by a few parts per billion of many volatile organic compounds is enough to render a supply unpotable for reasons of long-term health risks, even though the water may have no discernible taste or odor. The continuing discoveries of severe contamination in drinking water wells across the country only highlight the need for continued and expanded monitoring programs and bring home the necessity of preventing ground water pollution as the only reasonable protection to public health.

This chapter is based on Contamination of Ground Water by Toxic Organic Chemicals, a report written by the author while a staff member at the Council on Environmental Quality. Dated January 1981, the full text of the report is now available from the National Technical Information Service in Springfield, Virginia.

45

Ground Water Characteristics

Hydrologic Cycle

Ground water may be defined as subsurface water that occurs beneath a water table in soils or rocks or in geologic formations that are fully saturated (Freeze and Cherry, 1979). Aquifers, the subsurface permeable formations that contain ground water, underlie most of the nation. These formations can yield significant amounts of water to wells and springs. Ground water is a vast natural resource; its volume is estimated at about 50 times the annual flow of surface water (Davis, 1980). The U.S. Water Resources Council (USWRC) estimates that approximately 33-59 quadrillion gallons of fresh ground water (more than four times the volume of the Great Lakes) occur within one-half mile of the surface (USWRC, 1978a). Rainfall and snow melt recharge ground water at a rate of approximately 300 trillion gallons per year (Tripp and Jaffe, 1979) (one part recharge to 120 parts total volume). In the absence of human intervention, an equal volume of ground water would be recycled via evapotranspiration to the atmosphere or runoff into rivers and oceans.

Uses

Approximately 50% of all U.S. residents rely on ground water -- much of it untreated -- as a primary source of drinking water (USEPA, 1980). Drinking water uses about 18% of the fresh water withdrawn each year (USEPA, 1980). Ground water is relied upon for drinking water to different degrees throughout the nation, but more so in rural than in urban areas. The U.S. Environmental Protection Agency (USEPA) has estimated that 96% of all rural drinking water comes from ground water sources, in contrast to 20% of urban needs (Murphy, 1978).

Ground water supplies 25% of the fresh water used for all purposes in this country (USWRC, 1978b). Eight states (Arkansas, Mississippi, Texas, Nebraska, Iowa, Oklahoma, Florida, and Arizona) each rely on ground water for more than 60% of their total water use. According to 1975 data prepared by the U.S. Geologic Survey, ten states leading in intensity of ground water use ($m^3/day/km^2$) were, in order: California, Hawaii, New Jersey, Nebraska, Idaho, Kansas, Florida, Arkansas, Massachusetts, and Arizona. It is interesting to note that the water-rich eastern states of New Jersey and Massachusetts, which use substantial quantities of ground water for urban water supplies, outrank arid western states such as Arizona and Texas, where irrigation, rather than water consumption, is the predominant water demand.

Table 1. Fresh ground water use, 1950-1975[a]

Use	Percentage of total[b]			
	1950	1960	1970	1975
Irrigation	62	68	66	69
Industry	18	13	15	14
Public supplies	12	13	14	13
Rural supplies	8	6	5	5
Total withdrawals (trillion gallons per year)	12.4	18.3	24.8	29.9

[a]USEPA, 1980.

[b]Totals may not equal 100 because of rounding.

As shown in Table 1, approximately 30 trillion gallons of fresh ground water were withdrawn for all uses in 1975 -- for irrigation, 69%; industry, 14%; urban drinking water, 13%; and rural drinking water, 5%. Irrigated agriculture is the largest consumer of our water resources, accounting for over 50% of combined surface and ground water withdrawals and 80% of combined surface and ground water consumptive use. About 40% of irrigation water and approximately 57% of all water used for rural livestock comes from ground water sources.

In the 25 years from 1950 to 1975, the use of fresh ground water increased more than 140% (Table 1). The rate of ground water withdrawals has increased dramatically, averaging about 4% annually over the past 25 years. While the overall amount withdrawn in 1975 was an order of magnitude less than the total natural recharge (USEPA, 1980), local withdrawals often exceeded recharge, thereby creating overdrafts -- the long-term reduction of ground water also called ground water "mining." In 1975, approximately 25% of all ground water withdrawals were overdrafts, mostly in agricultural regions. For example, many areas such as the Texas High Plains, central Arizona, and southern Florida are experiencing declining water levels. It is common in these areas for the water table to drop 7-8 ft per year and the depth of pumping to be 6000 ft. With declining levels, ground water is often replaced with poor-quality water such as salt water or water containing undesirable minerals.

Protection by Soil Mantle

Ground water has always been thought of as a pristine resource, but recent surveys indicate that ground water is contaminated in many locations. Data show that this contamination, resulting most notably from organic and inorganic chemicals, originates from a variety of sources. Because ground water is widely used for drinking water, these toxic chemicals are being found in drinking water supplies, and they may pose unacceptable human health risks. Robert Harris will discuss these risks in Chapter 3.

In general, without prior contamination by human activity, most shallow or intermediate-depth ground water meets our intuitive notion and legal definition for acceptability as drinking water. Shallow ground water is usually of high quality because soils and soil microbes typically remove most of the conventional contaminants before the water reaches an aquifer. Cleansing by filtration and adsorption occurs as the water moves vertically and horizontally. With time, ground water tends toward chemical equilibrium with the minerals that it contacts, thereby increasing its mineral content. Fresh ground water may extend to depths of several thousand feet, but deep strata usually contain highly mineralized water known as brine. In some areas, even shallow ground water contains such high concentrations of specific ions or total dissolved solids that it is not fit for human or animal consumption or for irrigation.

Fundamentals of Ground Water Protection

As public officials and citizens consider the legal, institutional, and political complexities of protecting ground water from potential contamination, it is essential to keep a few physical, chemical, and biological concepts in mind.

First, ground water is vulnerable to contamination. Although filtration and adsorption cleanse many pollutants from percolating water, soil and rock strata do not eliminate most toxic chemicals. Plants and microorganisms, for example, do not break down many chlorinated hydrocarbons -- a class of resistant, nonbiodegradable, synthetic organic compounds. Moreover, once water reaches a saturated region, very little, if any, further cleansing takes place in a chemically reduced, abiotic, cool, and dark aquifer. Once contaminated, ground water may remain so for hundreds or thousands of years, if not for geologic time.

Second, the degree of threat to ground water depends on the materials underlying a surface site of potential contamination and the particular geologic and hydrologic conditions. In evaluating an existing or potential site, one must take into account (i) the hydrologic flow regime and

(ii) the types and thicknesses of soils both before and after the surface disturbance. For example, a lined, aqueous collection pond sited on a naturally occurring, thick clay layer is more secure than an unlined pit scooped from sandy soil.

Third, ground water moves slowly, typically less than a few tens-of-feet per year, depending on the hydraulic gradient and the permeability of the aquifer. A slug of contaminant moving with the ground water will flow and disperse into a plume, the dimensions of which are controlled by the structure of the aquifer. Because of the rate of travel and the vagaries of flow and dispersion, it may take decades for ground water that was polluted in one place to appear in a drinking water supply elsewhere. On the other hand, ground water may be heavily contaminated in one place, while only a few hundred feet away it may remain pristine.

Fourth, testing and monitoring are costly. Ground water sampling commonly requires expensive test wells and well casings. When ground water occurs in multiple layers between confining rock strata, several isolated test wells are needed. In fact, many wells are needed to locate and assess the rate of travel of a plume of contamination in most aquifers. Further assessment of quality requires sophisticated and expensive instrumentation. These measurements must be repeated regularly in order to follow migration.

Fifth, the qualities and quantities of ground and surface waters are interdependent. Fresh water wetlands commonly mark a hydrologic connection of surface and ground waters. Depending on the geology and hydrology of an area, contamination in a wetland or other surface water may pollute an aquifer, or vice versa.

Sources and Prevention of Contamination

The sources of toxic organic chemicals which can potentially contaminate ground water cannot be fully presented here. Suffice it to say that the sources discussed below represent primary contributors to ground water pollution.

- **Industrial Landfills**. Going back to the Industrial Revolution, but accelerating since World War II, large chemical companies have disposed of toxic organic chemicals in ways which cause many of our present problems (e.g., landfills, pits, holding ponds, and lagoons).

- **Municipal Landfills**. Leachates from municipal landfills have polluted a number of drinking water and ground water supplies.

- **Septic Tanks and Cesspools**. Many areas in the country, most notably Long Island's Nassau and Suffolk Counties, have problems arising from toxic organic chemicals used to clean septic tanks.

- **Mining and Petroleum Production**. These activities are often associated with environmental and ecological disruptions which cause major changes in the quantity and quality of adjacent ground water resources.

- **Agriculture**. The production and use of various pesticides have polluted major aquifers with carcinogenic or toxic contaminants, e.g., Aldicarb on Long Island, dibromochloropropane in California, and ethylene dibromide in Hawaii.

- **"Midnight Dumping"**. In the last few years, EPA has noted an increase in the volume of liquid hazardous wastes dumped along roadsides or into remote areas far from major population centers. These "midnight dumpers" do so for a variety of reasons, including the desire to avoid the high costs of proper and legal disposal. To the extent that generators of hazardous wastes cannot find easy and relatively inexpensive methods for proper disposal, "midnight dumpers" will pose a serious threat to the integrity of our ground water, marshes, and surface waters.

As the debate concerning ground water and hazardous wastes has unfolded in the newspapers and in Congress, more and more people have embraced the concept of prevention of contamination by permanent destruction, e.g., incineration of hazardous wastes and materials. Numerous incidents have proven beyond a doubt that long-term containment of hazardous wastes is difficult at best, and that restoration of a contaminated aquifer is impossible -- for both technical and economic reasons. Looking to the future, our society, institutions, and citizenry must realize that proper disposal (read, destruction) and prevention of contamination -- while not inexpensive -- are sound economic investments in terms of health and welfare.

Contamination of Drinking Water Wells

Recent Incidents of Contamination by Toxic Organic Chemicals

Contamination of ground water from human activities may come from surface impoundments, landfills, agriculture, leaks and spills, land disposal of waste waters, septic tanks, mining, petroleum, natural gas production, underground injection wells, and other sources. Recent data show that toxic organic chemicals contaminate public and private drinking water wells in many locations in all regions of the country. At best, some of these chemicals may have no detrimental effects at low concentrations. But many compounds, including some synthetic organic chemicals, can have serious and substantial health risks even at low concentrations, e.g., on the order of 10 ppb and below. To complicate the problem, many of these compounds are not easily detected during water consumption because they are tasteless and odorless. For most of the organic chemicals discussed here, there are no federal health standards for drinking water.

Ground water contamination by synthetic organic chemicals is particularly disturbing. Concentrations in ground water supplies are often orders of magnitude higher than those found in raw or treated drinking water drawn from the most contaminated surface water supplies. Data from several sources indicate contamination of drinking water wells by toxic organic chemicals in over 40 states. Surveys show that hundreds of wells supplying drinking water to millions of people have been closed because of high concentrations of these chemicals. Examples include:

● In late 1979, state health officials began to close contaminated private wells in Lake Carmel, New York, a community of relatively young families. By April 1981, the state had closed 32 private wells because the water contained hydrocarbons - organic chemicals, including benzene, a known cause of leukemia. For example, one young couple had their well declared unfit for drinking by the state in August 1979, but they continued to use it for bathing and washing clothes and dishes. The couple's four children, each then under five years of age, have suffered nagging health problems, including deep congestion, bronchial coughs, sore throats, skin rashes, diarrhea, chronic stomach aches, and urinary problems, according to their mother. The mother was hospitalized for suspected gall bladder trouble, and neighboring adults have had a variety of health problems, including high white blood cell count, painfully swollen joints, and "pigmentation of the kidney". The various adults attribute these health problems to drinking water from the contaminated wells before they were closed by the state. The local doctors "..(don't) know what it (the cause of the ailments) is...", or, "..they can't account for it..", according to two adults interviewed (Hanley, 1981).

● Over 9 million gallons of chemical wastes and hazardous solvents were poured into "Price's Pit", a 22-acre dump located 6 miles northwest of Atlantic City, New Jersey. The sandy, porous soil at the site allowed the chemicals to percolate rapidly to the ground water table, and the contamination seeped eastward with the flow of the Cohansey Aquifer at the rate of about 7 inches per day, or a half mile in ten years. By 1981, the contents of Price's Pit had caused the closure of 35 family wells in nearby Egg Harbor Township, but not before several major health problems and at least one premature death had occurred there. No one really knows if the contaminated water was responsible for the diseases and death, but no one can dispute that the tap water drunk by the people blackened pots, turned the laundry yellow, and at times fizzed like soda pop. By March 1982, state officials closed 7 municipal wells that had previously supplied approximately 40 percent of Atlantic City's tap water. City officials have now hired consultants and have worked with state and federal agencies to plan for the future (Grady, 1982).

● In January 1980, California public health officials closed 39 public wells supplying water to more than 400,000 people in 13 cities in the San Gabriel Valley because of trichloroethylene (TCE) contamination. (TCE is known to cause cancer in laboratory mice.) The pattern of contamination suggests multiple, widespread sources of the pollutant. The TCE concentration at one well, now closed, was 600 ppb (Schinazi, 1980).

● In South Brunswick, New Jersey, hazardous waste disposal activities contaminated the shallow aquifer. Until recently, a family living nearby relied on a private well for all domestic water. After a struggle with local and state health officials to have the water checked, independent chemical analyses showed that several toxic and/or carcinogenic compounds were present in high concentrations (Harris, 1979); they are shown in Table 2. Several neighbors´ wells also had high concentrations of these or similar contaminants (Brezenski, 1976).

● Rocky Mountain Arsenal, jointly operated for the Department of Defense by the U.S. Army Chemical Corps and Shell Chemical Company, is located between Denver and Brighton, Colorado. The facility disposed of complex chemical byproducts from the manufacture of pesticides and herbicides in unlined holding ponds, a practice which led to infiltration into the shallow water table aquifer and subsequent migration of contaminants through the ground water. Although this practice has been discontinued, 30 square miles of the shallow water aquifer are contaminated, resulting in abandonment of a number of domestic, stock, and irrigation wells. Soil near one pond is contaminated by the pesticides aldrin and dieldrin which bioaccumulate in the fatty tissues of organisms and persist in the environment for long periods (USEPA, 1980).

● In 1972, the Jackson Township, New Jersey, landfill was licensed by the state to accept sewage sludge and septic tank wastes. The landfill abuts the Ridgeway Branch of the Toms River and overlies the Cohansey Aquifer, the sole source of drinking water for the community. Approximately 100 drinking water wells around the landfill were closed because of organic chemical contamination, apparently from illegal disposal of chemicals in the landfill. Analyses of well water showed severe contamination (see Table 3). Residents believe that premature deaths, kidney malfunctions and nephrectomies, recurrent rashes, infections, and other health-related problems were caused by the contamination of

Table 2. Toxic organic pollution of a family well
in South Brunswick, New Jersey[a]

Chemical	Concentration (ppb)
Tricholoroethylene	1,530
Trichloroethane	965
Chloroform	420
Carbon tetrachloride	400
Xylenes	300
Toluene	260
Benzene	230
Dichloroethylene	58
Methylene chloride	11

[a]Brezenski, 1976.

Table 3. Toxic organic chemical pollution of drinking water
wells in Jackson Township, New Jersey[a]

Chemical	Concentration (ppb)
Toluene	6,400
Methylene chloride	3,000
Acetone	3,000
Ethyl benzene	2,000
Trichloroethylene	1,000
Benzene	330
Chloroform	33

[a]USEPA, 1980.

water supplies by the landfill.   The wells
have been closed (USEPA, 1980).

● In May 1978, four wells which provide 80% of
  the drinking water to Bedford, Massachusetts,
  were found to be contaminated with toxic
  organic chemicals, including up to 2100 ppb of
  dioxane and up to 500 ppb of TCE.   Officials
  do not know how long the water had been
  contaminated. The discovery was accidental,
  the result of a resident engineer's testing
  the water for a paper that he was writing.
  Local officials closed the wells, began water
  conservation measures, and purchased water (at
  retail prices) from four neighboring towns --
  until one of those towns was forced to close
  two of its main wells because of TCE
  contamination (Massachusetts Legislative
  Commission on Water Supply, 1979).

● Sixteen private drinking wells were closed in
  Gray, Maine, in 1977 after contamination with
  trichloroethane, TCE, freon, acetone, xylene,
  dimethyl sulfide, and various alcohols was
  discovered. All were located near an
  industrial waste handling facility built in
  1972 to process waste oil from the Tamano oil
  spill in Casco Bay. From then until 1977, the
  McKin Company used the facility as a transfer
  and processing station for approximately
  100,000-200,000 gallons of waste oil annually
  (USEPA, 1980).

These cases are from rural, suburban, and urban areas in large
and small, industrial and rural states. Although they suggest
that contamination is widespread, the lack of data makes a
thorough analysis difficult.

Ground Water Conditions and Trends

     There are no national synoptic data on ground water
contaminants, the number of persons exposed, or the health
effects sustained. These problems have only recently come to
public attention. With some exceptions, data on ground water
quality gathered by the states and the U.S. Geological Survey
do not generally focus on contamination from hazardous waste
disposal or on contamination by synthetic organic chemicals.
Whether available data reflect the range of water quality
problems is not known because, in almost every case studied to
date, only a few of several hundred possible compounds were

tested -- and then only when contamination was suspected.   In
some areas, re-analyses have shown high concentrations of
toxic substances not looked for the first time.

To gain a national perspective on the extent and severity
of ground water and drinking water contamination, the Council
on Environmental Quality (CEQ) collected detailed information
on drinking water from the ten EPA Regional Offices and many
states.   The Council sought information on the magnitude and
costs of problems, well closure, quality and quantity of
scientific data on the problems and closures, and health
effects in the populations served. The data available to the
Council left much to be desired in terms of depth, breadth,
accuracy, and precision.   But given that the ground water
pollution problem has only recently come to national attention
and the fact that measurements of the extent of contamination
are difficult and costly to make, this compilation   of
information provides the most comprehensive picture available.

The summary of CEQ findings is reported in Table 4.
There is no simple way to portray the data because of the lack
of a uniform reporting format. No attempt was made to show
the geographical extent of the problem or the number of other
states reporting similar problems with lower concentrations.
It is important to keep in mind that the highest
concentrations shown in Table 4 are probably reported in areas
that have been industrialized for many years or in states with
aggressive ground water monitoring programs. These data show
that at least one state in each of the ten EPA regions
reported significant problems. Almost all states east of the
Mississippi have major problems as do the relatively non-
industrial, lightly populated western states, e.g., Idaho,
Arizona, and New Mexico. For about one-half the states for
which problems were not reported, there are unconfirmed
newspaper reports of contamination problems -- for the most
part, discovered during or after the survey.

Certain low molecular weight chlorinated hydrocarbons
(solvents) appear to be most frequently responsible for
drinking well contamination. For example, trichloroethylene,
trichloroethane, tetrachloroethylene, carbon tetrachloride,
trifluorotrichloroethane, 1,1-dichloroethylene, 1,2-dichlo-
roethylene, and chloroform have been reported singly or
together in high concentrations in drinking water wells in
many states.

Concentrations of pollutants in drinking water from wells
may be contrasted with those in drinking water drawn from
surface water. The surface water concentrations in the last
column of Table 4 are considerably lower than those for

Table 4. Toxic organic compounds found in drinking water wells[a]

Chemical	Concentration (ppb)	State	Highest surface water concentration reported[a] (ppb)
Trichloroethylene (TCE)	27,300	Pennsylvania	
	14,000	Pennsylvania	
	3,800	New York	160
	3,200	Pennsylvania	
	1,530	New Jersey	
	900	Massachusetts	
Toluene	6,400	New Jersey	
	260	New Jersey	6.1
	55	New Jersey	
1,1,1-Trichloroethane	5,440	Maine	
	5,100	New York	5.1
	1,600	Connecticut	
	965	New Jersey	
Acetone	3,000	New Jersey	NI
Methylene chloride	3,000	New Jersey	
	47	New York	13
Dioxane	2,100	Massachusetts	NI
Ethyl benzene	2,000	New Jersey	NI
Tetrachloroethylene	1,500	New Jersey	
	740	Connecticut	21
	717	New York	
Cyclohexane	540	New York	NI
Chloroform	490	New York	
	420	New Jersey	700
	67	New York	
Di-n-butyl-phthalate	470	New York	NI

Table 4. (cont'd)

Chemical	Concentration (ppb)	State	Highest surface water concentration reported[a] (ppb)
Carbon tetrachloride	400	New Jersey	30
	135	New York	
Benzene	330	New Jersey	
	230	New Jersey	4.4
	70	Connecticut	
	30	New York	
1,2-Dichloroethylene	323	Massachusetts	
	294	Massachusetts	9.8
	91	New York	
Ethylene dibromide (EDB)	300	Hawaii	
	100	Hawaii	NI
	35	California	
Xylene	300	New Jersey	
	69	New York	24
Isopropyl benzene	290	New York	NI
1,1-Dichloroethylene	280	New Jersey	
	118	Massachusetts	
	70	Maine	0.5
1,2-Dichloroethane	250	New Jersey	4.8
Bis (2-ethylhexyl) phthalate	170	New York	NI
DBCP (Dibromochloropropane)	137	Arizona	
	95	California	NI
	68	California	
Trifluorotrichloroethane	135	New York	NI
	35	New York	

Table 4. (cont'd)

Chemical	Concentration (ppb)	State	Highest surface water concentration reported[a] (ppb)
Dibromochloromethane	55	New York	317
	20	Delaware	
Vinyl chloride	50	New York	9.8
Chloromethane	44	Massachusetts	12
Butyl benzyl-phthalate	38	New York	NI
gamma-BHC (Lindane)	22	California	NI
1,1,2-Trichloroethane	20	New York	NI
Bromoform	20	Delaware	280
1,1-Dichloroethane	7	Maine	0.2
alpha-BHC	6	California	NI
Parathion	4.6	California	0.4
delta-BHC	3.8	California	NI

[a]See report from CEQ, 1980 (pp. 36-39) for references for each of the state entries.

NI = Not investigated.

drinking water wells. In both relative and absolute terms, the contamination of drinking water supplies by toxic organic chemicals is worse for ground water supplies than surface water supplies. This conclusion runs counter to the previously unquestioned assumption that drinking water from ground water supplies can be used as a standard of purity in epidemiological and medical studies of human health.

Strengths and Weaknesses of the Data Bases

In reviewing the data bases used in this presentation, it is fair to say that the weaknesses surpass the strengths, if only due to the volume of our ground water resources and the number of potential contamination sites. In designing new surveys of ground water quality, reseachers must find ways to overcome formidable challenges:

- **Dispersed Wells and Spatial Variations.** Ground water monitoring wells supply data at only one x-y coordinate on the surface, and usually only at one depth. Thus many measurements from numerous (and expensive) wells are needed to piece together an areal "snapshot."

- **Temporal Variation.** Ground water flows, albeit slowly, so repeated measurements are needed to assemble time-series data.

- **Chemical Instrumentation.** Ground water samples require special collection and storage methods. Field instruments lack the sensitivity and reliability of laboratory analytic instruments, and certain laboratory instruments, e.g., gas chromatographs/mass spectrophotometers for measuring trace concentrations of volatile organic chemicals, require highly trained operators. Even then, measurements in the parts per billion range require great diligence, to ensure quality and correct interpretation of results.

- **Scope of Measurements.** Costs increase rapidly with the increasing number of potential contaminants. Often, one must make trade-offs between the number of different samples measured and the thoroughness of the measurements on each sample. For example, a commercial laboratory typically charges over $500.00 to measure the concentrations of organic chemicals now listed on EPA's "Priority Pollutant" list, but simple tests cost much less.

These challenges, and the general difficulties of field work, force the realization: citizens and officials will never have perfect scientific information upon which to make difficult decisions. Professional judgment as to "how much is enough" will always play a critical part of all decisions concerning ground water use, contamination, and protection.

Coda

Ground water is a vast natural resource of great economic importance to agriculture, industry, and everyday life. Twenty-five percent of all fresh water used in the United States comes from ground water supplies. One-half of all the people who reside in the United States rely on ground water as their source of drinking water. The rate of ground water use has risen much more rapidly in the last 25 years than total water usage. Because ground water lacks visibility, it is difficult to understand and easy to forget. Ignorance has led to abuse, and abuse to endangerment of critical supplies, in terms of both quantity and quality.

Ground water is easily contaminated, especially by certain volatile organic chemicals which readily penetrate the normal protective mechanisms. Once contaminated by organic chemicals -- even in concentrations of a few parts per billion -- ground water can no longer be used for drinking water, unless expensive treatment methods are installed. Some former drinking water supplies are so contaminated now that they may never be used again for many generations -- if ever. These hydrologic and biological realities are quite sobering. Having spent several years now understanding the intricacies of ground water management, I am glad to paraphrase the saw, "An ounce of prevention is worth a _ton_ of cure!"

References

Brezenski, F. T.   1976.   Laboratory   Director, U.S. Environmental   Protection   Agency,   Region II. Edison, New Jersey. Letter to W. Althoff, Department of Special Services, New Jersey Department of Environmental Protection. May 12, 1976.

Davis, S. T. 1980. Associate Assistant Administrator for Water and Waste Management. U.S. Environmental Protection Agency. Testimony before the Joint Hearing of the Subcommittee on Health and the Environment and the Subcommittee on Transportation and Commerce, House of Representatives. August 22, 1980.

Freeze, R. A., and J. A. Cherry. 1979. Groundwater. Prentice-Hall, Inc. Englewood Cliffs, New Jersey.

Grady, D. 1982. "Troubled Waters in Atlantic City." Discover, 76-80, March 1982.

Hanley, R. 1981. "Spread of Pollution Feared in Wells Around New York." New York Times, (Monday, April 6).

Harris, R. H. 1979. Staff scientist, Environmental Defense Fund. Memorandum and attachments to Ruffin Harris, October 12, 1979.

Massachusetts Special Legislation Commission on Water Quality, Massachusetts Department of Environmental Quality Engineering, and U.S. Environmental Protection Agency. 1979. Chemical Contamination. Boston.

Murphy, T. 1978. Deputy Assistant Administrator for Air, Land, and Water Use. U.S. Environmental Protection Agency. Testimony before the Subcommittee on the Environment and the Atmosphere and the Committee on Science and Technology, House of Representatives, April 26, 1978.

Schinazi, L. 1980. Regional Water Control Board. Los Angeles, California. Personal communication, September 1980.

Tripp, J.T.B., and A. B. Jaffe. 1979. "Preventing Groundwater Pollution: Toward a Coordinated Strategy to Protect Critical Recharge Zones." Harvard Environmental Law Review 3:3.

U.S. Environmental Protection Agency (USEPA). Office of Drinking Water. 1980. Planning Workshops to Develop Recommendations for a Ground Water Protection Strategy: Appendices. U.S. Government Printing Office, Washington, D.C.

U.S. Water Resources Council (USWRC). 1978. The Nation's Water Resources, 1975-2000, Volume 1: Summary. U.S. Government Printing Office, Washington, D.C.

Robert H. Harris

3. The Health Risks of Toxic Organic Chemicals Found in Groundwater

Introduction

The health significance of synthetic organic chemicals in drinking water has been under investigation since studies in 1974 suggested that drinking water from the lower Mississippi River in Louisiana increased the risk of gastrointestinal and urinary tract cancer (Page, Harris and Epstein, 1976). Through these, and numerous other studies evaluating certain exposures in the occupational setting, it has become clear that many synthetic organic chemicals once thought safe may present serious and substantial health risks even in concentrations in the low parts per billion (ppb) or parts per trillion (ppt) range. It has only been recently, however, that the concern for the presence of these chemicals in drinking water has been extended to include groundwater supplies.

At high concentrations and doses (acute exposures), many synthetic organic compounds can cause nausea, dizziness, tremors, blindness, or other health problems (Lewis and Tatken, 1980). At lower concentrations, skin eruptions may develop, or the central nervous system may be impaired. At still lower concentrations, over many months or years (chronic exposures), subtle health problems or problems that may be difficult to conclusively link with drinking water may emerge. With human or animal carcinogens, there is often a long latency between time of exposure and manifestation of disease (National Research Council, 1977; Russell, 1978).

Although many of the organic chemicals found in drinking water wells have been tested in the laboratory for acute and chronic toxicity, there is little evidence to implicate them with adverse human health effects except in certain occupational settings and in certain populations drinking chlorinated water. In a few locations (e.g. see the discussions of Gray, Maine; Bedford, Massachusetts; and Jackson Township, New Jersey, in the chapter by Burmaster) including Hardeman County, Tennessee, where groundwater is known to be contaminated with relatively high concentrations of certain organic chemicals, some people allege health damages ranging from skin rashes to cancer. Unfortunately, the alleged effects have not been rigorously evaluated although recent studies in Hardeman County are strongly suggestive of adverse health impacts. In fact, it may not be possible to determine with certainty whether the damages were even partly caused by contaminated drinking water. Retrospective studies of such incidents may not be conclusive because of inadequate data and the often small sample size. Nonetheless, anecdotal information together with the recent health studies in Hardeman County raise legitimate questions about the acute, subchronic and chronic effects that might result from consumption of contaminated groundwater.

Estimating Health Risks

Although it is not possible to predict with certainty the effects of drinking water contaminated with one or more of the organic compounds most often observed in contaminated groundwater (see Burmaster), crude estimates can be made. This section examines evidence from occupational exposures, from recent observations in Hardeman County, from epidemiological studies of populations drinking chlorinated water, and from laboratory studies of chemical carcinogens. Some of the evidence is difficult to interpret because of such unknown variables as individual smoking and alcohol consumption habits. Most of the evidence is difficult to generalize for lack of basic research. Although the compounds are manufactured and used widely, most have not been tested exhaustively for their toxic, mutagenic, teratogenic, or carcinogenic properties.

None of the synthetic organic compounds found in groundwater is known to benefit mammalian or human biochemistry, and each is known to be toxic in sufficiently high doses (Lewis and Tatken, 1980). For toxic compounds that do not show mutagenic, teratogenic, or carcinogenic activity, most toxicologists recommend that total exposures be kept below a specific daily or lifetime dose. Such dose limits are estimated from laboratory data and include a safety factor, usually ranging from 10 to 1,000, depending on the adequacy of the data and the circumstances of exposure (National Research Council, 1980).

For proven animal or human carcinogens, committees of the National Academy of Sciences and several federal and international health agencies assume no threshold of effect (National Research Council, 1980) -- that is, it is assumed that zero cancer risk occurs only at zero exposure. With sufficient laboratory data relating dose and response to a carcinogenic compound, it is sometimes possible to estimate total exposures that correspond roughly to stated levels of risk, a crude but plausible approach often taken in regulatory decisionmaking.

Evidence from Occupational Exposures

Scientists know a great deal about toxic effects of many substances based on studies of individuals exposed to relatively high doses at the workplace. In a sense, these workers form a natural, albeit unfortunate, experimental population. Sometimes it is possible to perform medical studies of these populations after a pattern of disease appears. With sufficient numbers of exposed persons and controls, statistical techniques can be used to identify a hazardous substance or a hazardous dose.

Several of the toxic organic compounds identified in groundwater have been the subject of occupational studies. A 1977 report of the National Institute for Occupational Safety and Health summarizes what is known about the systemic toxicity of these and other compounds (USDHEW, 1977). Information on the non-carcinogenic toxicity of 11 compounds frequently found in groundwater is condensed in Table 1. One of these compounds, vinyl chloride, is a human carcinogen.

Workers have manifested a variety of effects from exposure to high doses of the compounds, as shown in the table. Although biological transport and metabolism of a compound that is inhaled or absorbed through the skin may differ somewhat from that resulting from ingestion of the same compound, the systemic effects are expected to be similar. Many of the compounds depress the central nervous system, and/or cause dizziness, nausea, or fatigue. Several are known to damage the liver or kidneys. The immediate symptoms of many of the compounds are similar, and a physician may not be able to distinguish among them if a worker is exposed to several compounds.

Studies of occupational exposure have also shown that at high doses several of these compounds have adverse human reproductive effects. Table 2 summarizes the adverse reproductive effects associated with six chemicals

Table 1. Information on Noncarcinogenic Toxicity of 11 Chemicals Frequently Found in Groundwater

Chemical	Exposure	Systemic Effects
Trichloroethylene (TCE)	I,A	Acute exposure depresses the central nervous system, with such symptoms as headache, dizziness, vertigo, tremors, nausea and vomiting, irregular heart beat, sleepiness, fatigue, blurred vision, and intoxication similar to that from alcohol. Unconsciousness and death have been reported. Alcohol may worsen the symptoms and the worker may become flushed. Addiction and peripheral neuropathy have been reported.
1,1,1-Trichloroethane	I,A	Acts as a narcotic and depresses the central nervous system. Acute exposure symptoms include dizziness, incoordination, drowsiness, increased reaction time, unconsciousness and death.
1,1,2-Trichloroethane	I,A	No human toxic effects have been reported. In animals it is a potent central nervous system depressant. Injection of anesthetic doses in animals was associated with both liver and renal necroses.
Tetrachloroethylene	I,A	Acute exposure may cause central nervous system depression, hepatic injury, and anesthetic death. In animals it produces cardiac arrhythmias and renal injury. Symptoms of exposure include malaise, dizziness, headache, increased perspiration, fatigue, staggering gait, and slowing of mental ability.

Table 1, continued

Chemical	Exposure	Systemic Effects
1,2-Dichloroethylene	I	Acts primarily as a narcotic, causing central nervous system depression. Symptoms of acute exposure include dizziness, nausea and frequent vomiting, and central nervous system intoxication similar to that from alcohol. When renal effects occur, they are transient.
1,2-Dichloroethane	I,A	Inhalation of high concentrations may cause nausea, vomiting, mental confusion, dizziness, and pulmonary edema. Chronic exposure has been associated with liver and kidney damage.
Carbon Tetrachloride	I,A	Exposure may result in central nervous system depression and gastrointestinal symptoms of liver and kidney damage. Acute exposure symptoms include liver and kidney damage. Nausea, vomiting, abdominal pain, diarrhea, enlarged and tender liver, and jaundice result from liver damage. Diminished urinary volume, red and white blood cells in the urine, albuminaria, coma and death may result from acute kidney failure. Systemic effects worsen when used in conjunction with ingestion of alcohol.
Chloroform	I	A relatively potent anesthetic at high concentrations. Death from its use as an anesthetic has resulted from liver damage and from cardiac arrest. Exposure may cause lassitude, digestive disturbance, dizziness, mental dullness, and coma. Chronic overexposure can cause enlargement of the liver and kidney damage. Alcoholics seem to be affected sooner and more severely.

Table 1, continued

Chemical	Exposure	Systemic Effects
Dioxane	I,A	Exposure to vapor may cause drowsiness, dizziness, loss of appetite, headache, nausea, vomiting, stomach pain, and liver and kidney damage.
Vinyl Chloride	I	Depresses the central nervous system, with symptoms resembling mild alcohol intoxication. Lightheadedness, some nausea, and dulling of visual and auditory responses may develop in acute exposure. Death from severe exposure has been reported.
Toluene	I,A	Acute exposure results predominantly in central nervous system depression. Symptoms include headache, dizziness, fatigue, muscular weakness, drowsiness, incoordination with staggering gait, skin paresthesias, collapse, and coma.

I = Inhalation of gas or vapor.
A = Absorption through skin.

Source: U.S. Department of Health, Education and Welfare, Occupational Diseases: A Guide to Their Recognition (rev. ed.) (Washington, D.C., U.S. Government Printing Office, 1977), pp. 136-459.

for which there is some human evidence: dibromochloropropane (DBCP, now banned as a pesticide in the United
States), vinyl chloride, ethylene dibromide (EDB),
benzene, toluene, and xylene. Each has been proven to
have adverse human reproductive effects at high doses, and
for the first three, reproductive effects have also been
observed in at least one species of laboratory animal
(Clement Associates, 1981). However, there is no direct
human evidence to indicate whether exposure to these
chemicals at concentrations found in the most contaminated
groundwater is a significant hazard to human reproduction.

The data in Table 2 are qualitative only and are
difficult to extrapolate to the general population. In
most cases, either the exposure concentration in the
occupational setting is not known or, when it is known,
the dose-response data are inadequate to permit reliable
extrapolation to lower doses. Nonetheless, occupational
studies of the acute and subchronic effects of these
chemicals suggest -- at the least -- that reproductive
effects should not be ignored in any consideration of
health risks of these groundwater contaminants, particularly in heavily contaminated areas.

Evidence from Human Epidemiological Studies

During the past decade, levels of certain organic
contaminants in drinking water were measured and estimates
made of subsequent carcinogenic risks to humans. Much of
the initial work on cancer risks from drinking water
focused on chlorinated surface water which usually
contains varying amounts of four trihalogenated methanes
(THMs) -- chloroform, bromoform, bromodichloromethane, and
dibromochloromethane, in addition to other byproducts of
chlorination. The THMs are formed during chlorination by
the action of the chlorine on traces of bromide and
organic compounds consisting mainly of naturally occurring
organic chemicals called humic acids (Crump and Guess,
1980). The National Organics Reconnaissance Survey
(Symons et al, 1975) found that THM concentrations are
usually higher in chlorinated water and in drinking water
derived from chlorinated surface water than in drinking
water derived from chlorinated groundwater. (Surface
waters tend to have higher concentrations of natural
organic compounds that react with the chlorine to form
THMs and other compounds.) On the basis of this study,
unchlorinated groundwater is often regarded as the
standard for uncontaminated water and is often used as the
basis for comparison with waters from other sources.

Table 2. Chemicals Reportedly Associated with Adverse
          Reproductive Effects

Chemical	Sex	After occupational exposure
	Humans	
Dibromochloropropane (DBCP)	M	Infertility, azoospermia, decreased sperm counts
Vinyl Chloride	M	Chromosomal abnormalities, increased spontaneous abortion in wives of exposed workers.
Ethylene Dibromide (EDB)	M	Decreased fertility
Benzene, Toluene, Xylene	F	Prolonged menstrual bleeding

Chemical	Sex, species	Reported animal effects
	Animals	
Dibromochloro-propane (DBCP)	M rats, M rabbits, M guinea pigs	Atrophy and degeneration of testes
	F rat	Low birth weight in off-spring
Vinyl Chloride	F rat	Embryotoxicity, increased fetal mortality, increased hemorhages in fetuses
Ethylene Dibromide (EDB)	M rats, M cattle	Sterility
	F mouse	Low weights and increased skeletal abnormalities in fetuses

Source: Adapted from Clement Associates, Inc., Chemical
Hazards to Human Reproduction, prepared for the Council on
Environmental Quality (Springfield, VA: National Technical
Information Service, 1981, Tables IV-4, IV-5, VI-4, and
Appendix A.

The epidemiological evidence linking carcinogens in chlorinated drinking water with increased cancer risks has only limited usefulness in the context of evaluating the health risks posed by the mix of chemicals found in contaminated groundwater. Although a few of the same organic chemicals are present in both chlorinated surface water and contaminated groundwater, most of the compounds are different. For this reason, risk estimates for surface water cannot be directly applied to contaminated groundwater. Nonetheless, epidemiological studies of populations consuming chlorinated surface water provide important insights into the cancer risks associated with some chemicals and classes of chemicals found in groundwater. This may be true particularly for the chlorinated methanes and ethanes, which are ubiquitous contaminants of both chlorinated surface water and contaminated groundwater.

A number of epidemiological studies investigated the association between cancer and the presence of toxic organic chemicals in drinking water. The studies may be classified in two ways. "Ecological" studies compare cancer rates in groups of people to aggregate measures of exposure experienced by these groups. Primarily descriptive, the studies are useful in the formulation of hypotheses. "Case control" studies, on the other hand, usually relate exposures experienced by individuals with and without disease. They relate risk estimates to individual exposure patterns and are often used to test hypotheses suggested by ecological studies (Crump and Guess, 1980).

Until recently, ecological studies provided most of the evidence on the relationship between water quality and cancer. Most of the studies have been reviewed by Hoel and Crump (1979), Shy and Struba (1980), Wilkins, Reiches, and Kruse (1979), and the National Research Council (1980), all cited in Crump and Guess, 1980. The reports and their reviews suggest but do not claim to prove that an association has been demonstrated between either the chlorination of drinking water or presence of THMs and cancer mortality rates in several regions of the United States. Many of the ecological studies and the reviews suggest a positive association between a cancer -- often of the urinary tract or gastrointestinal system -- and the chlorination of drinking water or the presence of THMs.

Five recently completed case control studies investigated some of the hypotheses formulated in earlier ecological studies. Tables 3 and 4 summarize these major

Table 3. Case Control Study Summaries.

Site	Illinois	Louisiana	New York	North Carolina	Wisconsin
Authors	Brenniman et al. (1980)	Gottlieb et al. (1980)	Alavanja et al. (1978)	Struba (1979)	Kanarek and Young (1980)
Race	White	White/black	All	White/nonwhite	White
Sex	Male/female	Male/female	Male/female	Male/female	Female
Population	70 Illinois counties; 1973-76 deaths	20 south Louisiana parishes	7 upstate New York counties, 1968-70 deaths	North Carolina, 1975-78 deaths over age 45	Wisconsin 1972-77 deaths
Water variables	Ground only, chlor/unchlor.	Surface (Miss. R./ground), chlor/unchlor., surrogate for time on surface water, total chlorine, total organics	Chlor/unchlor., surface/ground	Surface/ground w/without contamination, treatment (none, pre-, post-chlor, both), previous use	Avg. water chlor. dose of 20 years ago, avg. pre-, post-chlor doses, exposure to rural runoff
Matching variables	None (case: control ratio = 1:14)[a]	Age, sex, race, parish group, some confounding deaths omitted.	Age, race, sex, for./U.S. born, yr. of death, county	Age, sex, race, 3 geoeconomic regions[b]	Age, year of death, county of residence

Table 3, continued.

Site	Illinois	Louisiana	New York	North Carolina	Wisconsin
Authors	Brenniman et al. (1980)	Gottlieb et al. (1980)	Alavanja et al. (1978)	Struba (1979)	Kanarek and Young (1980)
Other variables examined	Age, sex, urban/rural, SMSA/nonSMSA	Occupation, proximity to industrial site, Acadian ancestry	Urban/rural, occupation	Occupation, urbanization, socioeconomic status	Urbanization, occupation (<1% high risk), marital status
Mobility controls		4 categories by length of time on surface water	Study counties with low migration rate	Separate analysis for born and died in same county, born and died in N.C., died in N.C.	Study limited to 28 Wisconsin counties with 20-yr. migration rates <10%
Other special		Time-space clustering, numerous sub-studies	(+) Lung cancer risk found in urban chlor areas	Analyses for confounding and effect modification, migration, exposure-response gradients	Rural runoff and dose-response effects

Table 3, continued.

Site	Illinois	Louisiana	New York	North Carolina	Wisconsin
Authors	Brenniman et al. (1980)	Gottlieb et al. (1980)	Alavanja et al. (1978)	Struba (1979)	Kanarek and Young (1980)
Sites investigated and sample sizes[c]	Site specific for GI and UT	Rectum, colon urinary bladder kidney, liver, brain, pancreas, prostate	Site specific for GI and UT	Rectum, colon, urinary bladder	Site specific for GI, UT, brain, lung, breast
Principal results	(+) for colon and rectum in F and M & F combined, (+) for total GI tract (excluding liver) in F, (NS) for other sites	(+) for rectum, increasing risk ratios with increasing time on surface water and increasing proximity to mouth of Miss., (NS) for other sites	(+) for GI and UT cancers for chlor/unchlor in urban M and F	(+) chlor/unchlor and surface/ground for each of 3 sites in rural areas, bladder cancer typically showed largest odds ratios followed by rectum and then colon	(+) for colon with chlor, (NS) for colon cancer and with chlor in population not exposed to rural runoff, dose effect for chlor when rural runoff and water purification accounted for

(+) = odds ratios significantly greater than one at the level of $p < 0.05$
GI = gastrointestinal
UT = urinary tract
NS = not significant

Table 3, continued.

a. Some 43,666 controls were used at each site by Brenniman et al. Deaths excluded as controls were: congenital anomalies, perinatal causes, pregnancy complications, infectious diseases, mental disorders, senility.

b. Death certificates listing any cancer as a contributing cause were excluded from the controls by Struba. For colon and rectal cancer, death certificates indicating the presence of ulcerative colitis, familial polyposis coli, and adenomatous polyposis were also excluded from controls. Cases were excluded when it was not clear from available information whether the cancer at the site of interest was primary or metastatic.

c. Sample sizes for rectal, colon and bladder cancers are: Alavanja et al.: rectal – 393, colon – 1,064, bladder – 295 (the controls were matched one to one with cases); Brenniman et al.: rectal – 295, colon – 1,237, bladder – 284 (the same 43,666 controls were used for each site); Gottlieb et al.: rectal – 692, colon – 1,167, bladder – 759 (the controls were matched one to one with the cases); Kanarek and Young: rectal – 393, colon – 1,601, bladder – 230 (the controls were matched one to one with the cases); Struba: rectal – 702 (687 controls), colon – 1,484 (1,660 controls), bladder – 802 (801 controls).

Source: Kenny S. Crump and Harry A. Guess, Drinking Water and Cancer: Review of Recent Findings and Assessment of Risks, prepared for the Council on Environmental Quality by Science Research Systems Inc. (Springfield, VA: National Technical Information Service, 1980) pp. 28–31, based on M. Alavanja, I. Goldstein, and M. Susser, "Case Control Study of Gastrointestinal Cancer Mortality in Seven Selected N.Y. Counties in Relation to Drinking Water Chlorination," prepared for the U.S. EPA, Cincinnatti, 1978; G.R. Brenniman et al., "Case-Control Study of Cancer Deaths in Illinois Communities Served by Chlorinated or Nonchlorinated Water," in R.J. Jolley et al., eds., Water Chlorination Environmental Impact and Health Effects, Vol. 3 (Ann Arbor Science Publishers, 1980); M.S. Gottlieb, J.K. Carr, and D.T. Morris, "Cancer and Drinking Water in Louisiana: Colon and Rectum," to appear in International Journal of Epidemiology; M.S. Gottlieb, J.K. Carr, and J.R. Clarkson, "Drinking Water and Cancer in Louisiana: Mortality Study," submitted for publication; M.S. Kanarek and T.B. Young, "Drinking Water Chlorination and Female Cancer Mortality in Wisconsin, 1962–1977," prepared for The U.S. Environmental Protection Agency, 1980; and R.J. Struba, "Cancer and Drinking Water Quality," Ph.D. dissertation, University of North Carolina, 1979.

Table 4. Cancer Risk Ratios and 95 Percent Confidence Intervals (Chlorinated vs. Unchlorinated).

Site	Illinois	Louisiana	New York	North Carolina	Wisconsin
Authors	Brenniman et al. (1980)[a]	Gottlieb et al. (1980)[b,c]	Alavanja et al. (1978)[d]	Struba (1979)[b,c]	Kanarek and Young (1980)[e]
Rectum	1.26 crude (0.98, 1.61) 1.22 adjusted	1.41 (1.07, 1.87)	1.93 (1.32, 2.83)	1.53 (1.24, 1.89)	1.39 high (0.67, 2.86) 1.16 medium (0.58, 2.32) 1.13 low (0.61, 2.08)
Colon	1.08 crude (0.96, 1.22) 1.11 adjusted	1.05 (0.95, 1.18)	1.61 (1.28, 2.03)	1.30 (1.13, 1.50)	1.51 high (1.06, 2.14) 1.53 medium (1.08, 2.00) 1.53 low (1.11, 2.11)
Bladder	1.04 crude (0.81, 1.33) 0.98 adjusted	1.07 (0.84, 1.36)	1.69 (1.11, 2.56)	1.54 (1.26, 1.88)	1.04 high (0.43, 2.50) 1.03 medium (0.42, 2.54) 1.06 low (0.60, 3.09)

Table 4, continued.

a. Calculated for Caucasians of both sexes. Adjusted values were adjusted for age, sex, urban/rural, and SMSA/nonSMSA. Confidence intervals were not stated in original report; they were calculated by applying formulas in Fleiss to data on total cases and total controls.

b. Calculated for both sexes and all races combined.

c. Struba and Gottlieb et al. also computed odds ratios for surface water versus groundwater. These ratios are different from the ratios shown in this table and are listed here for comparison. The ratios and confidence intervals obtained by Struba are: rectum - 1.55 (1.26, 1.91), colon - 1.27 (1.10, 1.46), bladder - 1.48 (1.22, 1.80). Those obtained by Gottlieb et al. are: rectum - 1.51 (1.21, 1.90), colon - 0.95 (0.88, 1.03), bladder - 1.08 (0.87, 1.33).

d. Calculated for both sexes and all races combined. Confidence intervals were not stated in Alavanja et al. They were calculated by applying the method in Fleiss (1979) to data in Alavanja et al. (1977).

e. Calculated for white females and for high, medium and low average daily chlorine doses compared to no chlorination. Odds ratios and confidence intervals were computed by logistic regression, controlling for urbanization, marital status, and site-specific occupation.

Source: Kenny S. Crump and Harry A. Guess, 1980; M. Alavanja, I. Goldstein, and M. Susser, 1978; G.R. Brenniman, 1980; M.S. Gottlieb, J.K. Carr and D.T. Morris (submitted for publication); M.S. Gottlieb, J.K. Carr and J.R. Clarkson (submitted for publication); M.S. Kanarek and T.B. Young, 1980; R.J. Struba, 1979; J.L. Fleiss, 1979.

studies of populations in New York, Illinois, Wisconsin, Louisiana, and North Carolina.

In each case control study, death certificates were used to locate the home addresses of individuals who died from gastrointestinal or urinary tract cancers. Water supplies serving the addresses were then identified and their chlorination status (chlorinated or unchlorinated) and source (surface or groundwater) determined. Comparable information was obtained for deaths from other causes. In most of the studies, the control population and cancer victims were matched by sex, race, age, and year of death (Crump and Guess, 1980). With this information for each type of cancer, the ratio of the cancer risk for those who drank chlorinated vs. unchlorinated water was estimated (Crump and Guess, 1980). In four of the five studies, the risk ratios for surface and groundwaters were also computed. All five studies attempted to account for the influence of urbanization, occupation, and other confounding risk factors. Most of these studies also attempted to account for population migration.

Increased rectal, colon, and bladder cancer risk ratios were found by several investigators in several areas. The risk ratios for these cancers are large enough to be of concern, yet small enough to be difficult to study using epidemiological techniques (Crump and Guess, 1980).

The five case control studies found rectal cancer risks associated with chlorinated water to be a factor of 1.13-1.93 higher than those associated with unchlorinated water. In three studies (New York, Louisiana, North Carolina), the elevation in risk ratios was statistically significant. Colon cancer risk ratios also exhibited statistically significant elevations above 1.00 in three of the studies (New York, Wisconsin, North Carolina), as did bladder cancer risk ratios in two of them (New York, North Carolina).

Three of the studies (Louisiana, Wisconsin, North Carolina) looked for dose-response effects to see whether cancer risks increased with increasing exposure to organic contaminants in drinking water. No clear trend was evident. The Louisiana study showed increasing rectal cancer mortality rates with increasing exposure to surface water, a fact that suggests a dose-response gradient for rectal cancer; among those drinking water from the Mississippi River, the risk increased with increasing proximity to the mouth of the River. In the Wisconsin study, a colon cancer dose-response gradient was suggested when water purification and rural runoff were taken into account (Crump and Guess, 1980).

Although the methods used in these case control studies are a considerable refinement over those used in earlier ecological studies, the case control studies still possess some of the same limitations as the ecological studies. In both types, essentially the same indirect measures of water quality were used. Information on dietary and smoking habits was not available from death certificates. Death certificates include only a recent home address and the usual occupation; detailed residential and occupational histories are not available. In addition, the time between exposure to a carcinogen and diagnosis is probably at least 10 years for gastrointestinal and urinary tract cancers. Thus the water qualities which should be correlated with increased cancer risks in these studies are those to which the subjects were exposed at least 10 years before death. None of the studies includes direct measurements of water quality.

Nevertheless, the case control studies completed in the last 3 years have considerably strengthened the evidence linking elevated risks of lower gastrointestinal and urinary tract cancers with chlorinated drinking water. As discussed above, however, these data are of only limited usefulness in the quantification of health risks associated with the high concentrations of contaminants recently found in some drinking water wells. The range of the concentrations of chlorination byproducts (typically less than several hundred parts per billion) in surface water is frequently exceeded by the concentrations of some of the same or similar carcinogens found in contaminated groundwater (see Burmaster), thus suggesting that contaminated groundwater may present a significant cancer risk if ingested over a lifetime. Whether the cancer risks associated with contaminated groundwater wells equal or exceed the risks associated with chlorinated drinking water from surface sources may remain unknown indefinitely unless extensive epidemiological investigations of populations exposed to contaminated groundwater are undertaken.

Evidence from Animal Studies of Carcinogenicity

As discussed above, epidemiological studies do not permit quantitative estimates of the human health risks from exposure to the organic contaminants in unchlorinated groundwater. However, for a number of the contaminants for which carcinogenicity studies have been completed, there are adequate dose-response data from animal experiments to permit crude human risk estimates. It must be emphasized here that there is considerable uncertainty and debate regarding application of animal bioassays to human cancer risk estimates. The following calculations are rough estimates of cancer risks, and they must be interpreted carefully in light of the uncertainties.

The carcinogenic properties of the most frequently observed groundwater contaminants have been reviewed and the lifetime cancer risks associated with lifetime consumption are estimated from animal bioassay data (Crump and Guess, 1980). First, low-dose carcinogenic risks were estimated from animal data by a multistage method recently adopted by the Environmental Protection Agency (Federal Register, 1980). Then the animal risk estimates were extrapolated to humans by use of a method based on the relative surface areas of the animal and humans. The calculated cancer risks were then used to estimate 95 percent and 99 percent upper confidence limits[1] on risks for the chemicals found in drinking water wells.

There are many uncertainties associated with this procedure which could lead to either over- or underestimation of risks. The true dose-response relationship may be nonlinear, or the relative surface area concept may not accurately reflect relative potency of carcinogens in humans and animals. It is also possible that the contaminants could act synergistically with each other and with other carcinogens in the human environment; the carcinogenic effect could be larger than any suggested by animal studies of single chemicals. No data are available from which the risks associated with multiple exposures can be estimated accurately. Further, underestimation could arise because chemicals without an adequate dose-response data base can not be considered in a risk analysis.

---

[1]Numerical values (estimates of 95 percent upper confidence limits) are used in this report in the assessment of the probable upper bounds for carcinogenic risks. The statistical techniques used to estimate these upper bounds take into account statistical variations in the experimental data. They do not take into account variance from other sources, such as the unknown amount of variance arising from key assumptions in the model specification and extrapolation procedures.

For all but 2 of the 33 compounds (acetone and ethyl benzene) listed by Burmaster (Chapter 2), evidence of carcinogenicity was reviewed (Crump and Guess, 1980); this review is summarized in Table 5. For benzene and vinyl chloride, there is evidence of human carcinogenicity from epidemiological studies (Tomatis, 1979, as cited in Crump and Guess, 1980). Fifteen of the remaining chemicals have been tested for carcinogenicity in animal bioassays. The animal data for 1,1,1-trichloroethane were negative in the first animal bioassay study (recent unpublished data, however, suggest that this chemical is carcinogenic to mice), and the data for 1,1-dichloroethane and parathion are only suggestive. The remaining 12 chemicals are considered carcinogenic in at least one animal species. These classifications are based upon the original investigators' judgments.

Risk estimates were calculated with the multistage surface-area method, which, it can be argued, provides a reasonable upper bound on the human risks from exposure to these carcinogens. Table 6 presents upper confidence limits for the human cancer risk of water containing 1 ppb, assuming, as the National Research Council did in 1977 (National Research Council, 1977) that a person weighs 70 kg and consumes 2 liters of water per day. Estimates for benzene were based on human data. Each estimate was made for the species-sex-tumor site category which provided the largest risk estimate.

The risk esimates presented in Table 6 assume a linear relationship between dose and cancer incidence at low doses and allow for the possibility of a nonlinear relationship at higher doses. Upper statistical confidence limits computed with the multistage model vary linearly with those at low doses, and thus can be expected to provide reasonable upper limits on risks at low doses.

Calculation of potential lifetime cancer risks for a private drinking water well near Princeton, New Jersey, illustrates how one would use the risk estimates in Table 6. This well is typical of one contaminated by leachate from a hazardous waste landfill; it does not represent a "worst case" example. Table 7 shows concentrations of 9 organic chemicals detected in the New Jersey well and their associated lifetime cancer risk. Assuming that the cancer risks are simply additive, the risk of cancer from lifetime consumption of water from this well is 5.49×10^{-3} -- approximately 1 in 200. Stated another way, if a population of 1 million were to consume this water for a

Table 5.   Selected Synthetic Organic Chemicals Detected
           in Drinking Water Wells

Chemical	Evidence for carcinogenicity
Benzene	H
alpha-BHC	CA
beta-BHC	NTA
gamma-BHC (Lindane)	CA
Bis (2-ethylhexyl) phthlate	NTA
Bromoform	NTA
Butyl benzyl phthalate	NTA
Carbon tetrachloride	CA
Chloroform	CA
Chloromethane	NTA
Chlorohexane	NTA
Dibromochloropropane (DBCP)	CA
Dibromochloromethane	NTA
1,1-Dichloroethane	SA
1,2-Dichloroethane	CA
1,1-Dichloroethylene	NTA
1,2-Dichloroethylene	NTA
Di-n-butyl phthalate	NTA
Dioxane	CA
Ethylene dibromide (EDB)	CA
Isopropyl benzene	NTA
Methylene chloride	CA
Parathion	SA
Tetrachloroethylene	CA
Toluene	NTA
1,1,1-Trichloroethane	NA
1,1,2-Trichloroethane	CA
Trichloroethylene (TCE)	CA
Trifluorotrichloroethane	NTA
Vinyl chloride	H, CA
Xylene	NTA

 H = Confirmed human carcinogen.
CA = Confirmed animal carcinogen.
SA = Suggested animal carcinogen.
NA = Negative evidence of carcinogenicity from animal
     bioassay.
NTA = Not tested in animal bioassay.

    Source: Adapted from Kenny S. Crump and Harry A.
Guess, Drinking Water and Cancer: Review of Recent Findings
and Assessment of Risks, prepared for the Council on
Environmental Quality by Science Research Systems, Inc.
(Springfield, VA: NTIS, 1980), pp. 48-49.

Table 6. Estimated Upper Statistical Confidence Limits on Cancer Risks from Lifetime Consumption of Water Containing 1 ppb of a Given Chemical.

Chemical	Limits 95%	Limits 99%	Sex, Species	Tumor Type
Benzene	$^a 4.4 \times 10^{-6}$		Human	Leukemia
alpha-BHC	3.5×10^{-6}	8.0×10^{-6}	M rat	Hepatocellular carcinoma
gamma-BHC	1.3×10^{-5}	1.6×10^{-5}	M mouse	Hepatocellular carcinoma (pooled controls)
Carbon tetrachloride	1.9×10^{-6}	2.2×10^{-6}	M mouse	Hepatocellular carcinoma
Chloroform	4.1×10^{-6}	4.4×10^{-6}	F mouse	Hepatocellular carcinoma
Dibromochloropropane (DBCP)	2.0×10^{-4}	2.2×10^{-4}	M rat	Squamous cell carcinoma of the stomach
1,1-Dichloroethane	1.5×10^{-4}	1.9×10^{-4}	M mouse	All malignant tumors
1,2-Dichloroethane	1.0×10^{-6}	1.2×10^{-6}	M rat	Hamangiosarcoma of circulatory system
Dioxane	3.9×10^{-7}	4.4×10^{-7}	M rat	Nasal squamous cell carcinoma
Ethylene dibromide (EDB)	4.8×10^{-4}	5.4×10^{-4}	M rat	Squamous cell carcinoma of forestomach
Parathion	2.9×10^{-5}	3.6×10^{-5}	F rat	Adrenal cortical adenoma or carcinoma
Tetrachloroethylene	9.3×10^{-7}	1.0×10^{-6}	M mouse	Hepatocellular carcinoma

Table 6, continued.

Chemical	Limits 95%	Limits 99%	Sex, Species	Tumor Type
1,1,2-Trichloroethane	1.6×10^{-6}	2.0×10^{-6}	M mouse	Hepatocellular carcinoma
Trichloroethylene (TCE)	3.0×10^{-7}	3.3×10^{-7}	M mouse	Hepatocellular carcinoma
Vinyl chloride	4.1×10^{-6}	4.6×10^{-6}	M, F rat	Liver angiosarcoma

a. Point estimate.

Source: Adapted from Kenny S. Crump and Harry A. Guess, Drinking Water and Cancer: Review of Recent Findings and Assessment of Risks, prepared for the Council on Environmental Quality by Science Research Systems, Inc. (Springfield, VA: National Technical Information Service, 1980), pp. 60-61; N. Ito, et al., "Brief Communication: Development of Hepatocellular Carcinomas in Rats Treated with Benzene Hexachloride," Journal of the National Cancer Institute, 54:801 (1975); N. Maltoni, "Vinyl Chloride Carcinogenicity: An Experimental Model for Carcinogenesis Studies," in H.H. Hiatt, J.E. Watson, and J.A. Winsten, eds., Origins of Human Cancer (Cold Springs Harbor Lab., NY, 1977); and publications of the National Cancer Institute: Bioassay of Tetrachloroethane for Possible Carcinogenicity, Tech. Rep. Series 2, CAS 79-01-6, NCI-CG-TR-2; Report on the Carcinogenesis Bioassay of Chloroform (Springfield, VA: NTIS, 1976); Bioassay of Lindane for Possible Carcinogenicity, CAS 58-89-9, NCI-CG-TR-14; Bioassay of Tetrachloroethane..., CAS 127-18-4, NCI-CG-TR-13; Bioassay of Dibromochloropropane..., CAS 96-12-8, NCI-CG-TR-28; Bioassay of 1,1-Dichloroethane..., CAS 75-34-3 (1978); Bioassay of 1,2-Dichloroethane..., CAS 107-06-2, NCI-CG-TR-55 (1978); Bioassay of 1,4-Dioxane..., CAS 112-91-1, NCI-CG-TR-80; Bioassay of 1,2-Dibromoethane..., CAS 106-93-4, NCI-CG-TR-86; Bioassay of 1,1,2-Trichloroethane..., CAS 79-00-5, NCI-CG-TR-74 (1978); Bioassay of Parathion..., CAS 56-38-2, NCI-CG-TR-70 (1979).

Table 7.   Organic Chemicals Detected in a Highly Polluted
           New Jersey Well.

Chemical	Concentration (ppb)	Upper Limits on lifetime cancer risks[a]
Trichloroethylene (TCE)	1,530	4.6×10^{-4}
Trichloroethane	965	15.4×10^{-4} [b]
Chloroform	420	17.2×10^{-4}
Carbon tetrachloride	400	7.6×10^{-4}
Xylenes	300	No positive data
Toluene	260	No positive data
Benzene	230	10.1×10^{-3}
Dichloroethylene	58	No positive data
Methylene chloride	11	Risk estimates not yet available.

a. Calculated using 95 percent upper limits in Table 7.

b. Assuming the 1,1,2-trichloroethane isomer.

Source: Kenney S. Crump and Harry A. Guess, Drinking
Water and Cancer: Review of Recent Findings and Assessment
of Risks, prepared for the Council on Environmental Quality
by Science Research Systems, Inc., (Springfield, VA: National
Technical Information Service, 1980), p. 73.

lifetime, an additional 5,490 people would contract cancer in their lifetime.

It is interesting to note that the cancer risks associated with chlorinated water appear to be considerably greater than the risks estimated for the contaminated well in New Jersey based on extrapolation of animal data. However, a number of caveats are appropriate. First and foremost, however crude, the risk estimate for New Jersey groundwater pertains to the lifetime cancer risks for a single well. Second, evidence suggests that the risk estimates derived from animal data are underestimates of the true cancer risks (Crump and Guess, 1980). Third, there are no data to suggest how two or more compounds might interact; the calculation is based on an assumption of purely additive effects. Fourth, four of the compounds have not been adequately tested for their carcinogenicity, and other carcinogens may be present but undetected in the limited testing of the well. Thus, it is not possible to ascertain the true cancer risk associated with drinking water from this well.

Early Warnings from Hardeman County

In the early 1960's, pesticides leaking from a Memphis landfill were alleged to be responsible for major fish kills along the Mississippi River south of Memphis. As a result, Velsicol Chemical Corporation, a major contributor to that landfill, transferred its waste disposal operations to Toone-Teague Road in rural Hardeman County, some 60 miles east of Memphis. Using what Velsicol termed the "time-honored practice [of] shallow burial of toxic wastes", over 300,000 55-gallon drums of solid and liquid pesticide production wastes were buried in trenches at the site between 1964 and 1972, when the State ordered the dumping stopped.

Hydrogeological studies in 1967 concluded that groundwater was flowing in a direction away from the local private drinking water wells (Rima, et al., 1967). Nonetheless, by 1977 local residents were complaining of taste and odor in their well water and reporting an unusually high number of symptoms. These included skin and eye irritation, weaknesses in the upper and lower extremities; upper respiratory infection; shortness of breath; and severe gastrointestinal symptoms, including nausea, diarrhea, and abdominal cramping (Clark, et al, 1982). Unfortunately, the early hydrogeological studies were wrong -- pesticide waste had slowly been seeping into wells and was contaminating drinking water with extraordinarily high concentrations of a number of toxic and known carcinogenic chemicals (e.g. carbon tetrachloride, chloroform, and tetrachloroethylene) in addition to a number of other chemicals that may represent a chronic health threat (Table 8).

In 1978, a medical team from the University of Cincinnatti Medical Center (Clark et al., 1982) conducted an environmental health survey of the residents and a control group to determine if any adverse health effects resulting from exposure to the toxic compounds in the well water could be found. The survey utilized a health questionnaire, a clinical examination, and a biochemical screening. Preliminary studies were conducted in November, 1978, when many residents were still using the water for washing and toilet use (most had stopped using the water for drinking and cooking by May, 1978). Follow-up studies were conducted in January, 1979, when practically all residents had stopped using the contaminated well water for all uses.

The November survey indicated a high incidence of abnormal liver function in the exposed group compared to the controls; by January, the differences were not statistically significant suggesting transitory liver injury. However, during physical examinations in January, 6 individuals out of 48 examined in the exposed group and 1 individual out of 24 in the intermediate-exposed group (none in the 46 controls) had borderline liver enlargement. This finding led the investigators to conclude that, "... the most likely reason for the presence of abnormalities discovered in the inhabitants of the Toone-Teague Road area was the consumption of water from wells contaminated by the leaching of materials from the chemical land dump located in that area." (Clark et al., 1982).

More recently, Dr. Robert Rhamy of the Vanderbilt University Medical School (Rhamy et al., 1982) conducted complete histories and physical examinations of 112 people living or formerly living within a three mile area of the Velsicol dump site. During the period of exposure (approximately 1971-1978), a majority of those interviewed experienced a wide range of acute symptoms including: headaches, faintness, and dizziness; burning of the eyes, bloodshot eyes, and photophobia; burning in the nose and throat; shortness of breath; nausea; tingling and paresthesias, muscular weakness; and lassitude. Physical examinations revealed that 28% of those exposed suffered diastolic hypertension, 8% increased liver size, 11% optic

Table 8.   Contaminants Detected* in Private Wells Serving
            Exposed Residents in Toone-Teague Area of Hardeman
            County, Tennessee (as reported by Clark, et al.)

Compound	NP/NT†	Range (µg/L)	Median (µg/L)
Benzene	7/7	5-15	12
Carbon Tetrachloride	15/15	61-18,700	1,500
Chlordene	5/24	Trace-0.81	Trace
Chlorobenzene	23/25	Trace-41	5.0
Chloroform	14/15	2.1-1,890	140
Hexachlorobutadiene	22/28	Trace-2.53	0.15
Hexachloroethane	19/31	Trace-4.6	0.26
Hexachlorobicyclo-heptadiene (HEX-BCH)	24/31	Trace-2.2	0.05
Methylene Chloride	11/11	1.5-160	45
Napthalene	13/13	Trace-6.7	ND§
Tetrachloroethylene	27/28	Trace-2,405	3.5
Toluene	14/24	0.1-52	0.6
Xylenes	2/3	0.07-1.6	0.07

*U.S. Environmental Protection Agency, Region IV.   March 9,
 1979.   Summary of USEPA and State of Tennessee Chemical
 Analysis, Atlanta, Georgia.

†NP = Number of samples with detectable amounts of the
      substance tested;
 NT = total number of samples tested.

§ND = not detected.

atrophy, 18% peripheral neological changes, and 32% suffered significant eye problems. Although no controls were examined in this study, Rhamy tentatively concluded that these health problems were related to exposures from the contaminated well water.

Although the studies by Clark et al. (1982) and Rhamy (1982) do not conclusively prove that the residents along Toone-Teague Road were adversely affected by the contaminated groundwater, data on systemic toxicity of several of the contaminants, coupled with the high exposure levels found in Hardeman County, support these findings. In addition to the acute and subchronic effects of these exposures, chronic effects, including cancer, must be considered a distinct possibility. However, because a latency of ten or more years is usually observed between first exposure and clinical manifestations of a tumor, the relatively short time since first exposure (estimated somewhere between 1970-72), suggests that it may not yet be possible to observe a statistically significant increase in the risk of cancer. Therefore, to estimate these risks, reliance must be made on epidemiological studies conducted elsewhere and on risk estimates derived from laboratory bioassay studies, as discussed above.

Conclusions

Several of the organic chemicals detected in contaminated groundwater have been tested in laboratory animals for their possible acute and chronic toxicities. There is little evidence to implicate them in the impairment of human health, except for health impacts observed following high exposures to some of the chemicals in certain occupational settings and in certain populations drinking chlorinated water. However, preliminary health studies of the population exposed to heavily contaminated groundwater in Hardeman County, Tennessee, suggest a relationship between both transitory and irreversible health damage and organic chemicals in groundwater.

Because adequate epidemiological studies have not been made on populations consuming contaminated groundwater, potential adverse health risks must be inferred from evidence from occupational exposures, from epidemiological studies of populations drinking chlorinated water, and from the effects of toxic organic chemicals on laboratory animals. Although occupational experience with several of these chemicals has demonstrated acute, subchronic and chronic health effects, the data are inade-

quate to permit reliable extrapolation to populations
consuming contaminated groundwater.

Despite the considerable number of epidemiological
studies conducted since 1974 on the cancer risks of
carcinogens in drinking water, their usefulness in
assessing the risks posed by groundwater contaminants is
limited. The epidemiological evidence suggests that
chlorinated drinking water increases the risks of rectal,
colon, and bladder cancers. However, the mix of carcinogens and potential carcinogens (e.g., trihalomethanes and
unspecified nonvolatile halogenated organic compounds)
resulting from the addition of chlorine to drinking water
is distinctly different from the mix of carcinogens in the
groundwater pollution incidents discussed by Burmaster.
The assessment of risks from one cannot be directly
applied to the other.

For a number of the carcinogens identified in
contaminated groundwater, dose-response data from laboratory animal experiments permit crude human risk estimates.
It must be noted that these risk estimates are subject to
uncertainties, including the validity of the multistage
model, the method of extrapolation from animals to humans,
the possible synergistic effects of carcinogens in the
water with each other and with other carcinogens to which
humans are exposed, and the possible presences of carcinogens which have not yet been identified in the water.

References

Clarke, C.S., C.R. Meyer, P.S. Gartside, V.A. Majeti, B.
    Specker, W.F. Balistresi and V.J. Elia, 1982, "An
    Environmental Health Survey of Drinking Water
    Contamination by Leachate from a Pesticide Waste Dump
    in Hardeman County, Tennessee", Arch. Environ.
    Health. 37:9-18.

Clement Associates, Inc., 1981, Chemical Hazards to Human
    Reproduction, prepared for the Council on Environ-
    mental Quality, National Technical Information
    Service, Springfield, Virginia.

Crump, K.S. and H.A. Guess, 1980, Drinking Water and
    Cancer: A Review of Recent Findings and Assessment of
    Risks, prepared for the Council on Environmental
    Quality, National Technical Information Service,
    Springfield, Virginia.

Federal Register, 1980, "Water Quality Criteria Documents: Availability". Environmental Protection Agency. Vol. 45, No. 231:79318-79379.

Hoel, D.G. and K.S. Crump, 1979, "Scientific Evidence of Risks from Water-Borne Carcinogens", in Scientific Basis of Health and Safety Regulations, Brookings Institute, Washington, D.C.

Lewis, R.J., Sr., and R.L. Tatken (eds.), 1980, Registry of Toxic Effects of Chemical Substances, 2 vols. U.S. Government Printing Office, Washington, D.C.

National Research Council, Safe Drinking Water Committee, 1977, Drinking Water and Health, National Academy of Sciences, Washington, D.C.

National Research Council, 1980, Drinking Water and Health, vol. 3, National Academy Press, Washington, D.C.

Page, T., R.H. Harris, and S.S. Epstein, 1976, "Drinking Water and Cancer Mortality in Louisiana", Science. 19:55-57.

Rhamy, R.K., Professor Emeretis, Vanderbilt University Medical School. 1982, personal communication.

Rima, D.R., E. Brown, D.F. Goerlitz and L.M. Law, 1967, Potential Contamination of the Hydrologic Environment From the Pesticide Waste Dump in Hardeman County, Tennessee. U.S. Geological Survey.

Russell, C.S. (ed.), 1978, Safe Drinking Water: Current and Future Problems, Resources for the Future, Washington, D.C.

Shy, C.M., and R.J. Struba,1980, Cancer Epidemiology and Prevention (D. Schottenfield and J. Fraumeni, Jr., eds). W.B. Saunders Co., Philadelphia, Pennsylvania.

Symons, J.M., Thomas A. Bellar, T. Keith Carswell, Jack DeMarco, Kenneth L. Kropp, Gordon G. Robeck, Dennis R. Seeger, Clois J. Slocum, Bradford L. Smith, and Alan A. Stevens, 1975, "National Organic Reconnaisance Survey for Halogenated Organics", Journal of American Water Works Association. 67:634-647.

Tomatis, L., 1979, "The Predictive Values of Rodent Carcinogenicity Tests in the Evaluation of Human Risks".

92   *Robert H. Harris*

Annual *Review* *of* *Pharmacology* *and* *Toxicology.* 19:511-530.

U.S. Department of Health, Education and Welfare, 1977, *Occupational* *Diseases:* *A* *Guide* *to* *Their* *Recognition,* (rev. ed.), U.S. Government Printing Office, Washington, D.C.

Wilkins, J.R. III, N.A. Reiches, and C.W. Kruse, 1979, "Organic Chemicals in Drinking Water and Cancer", *American* *Journal* *of* *Epidemiology.* 110:420-48.

David W. Miller

4. Protection of Groundwater Quality

Introduction

Groundwater is the source of drinking water for approximately half of the population of the United States. Except for chlorination, it is rarely treated, presumed to be naturally protected, and considered free of the impurities associated with surface waters because it comes deep from within the earth. There are tens of thousands of community water supply wells and millions of domestic wells in the nation. Until the Federal Safe Drinking Water Act (SDWA) was passed in 1974, there was no formalized national program for analyzing potential toxic elements in public water supplies, including groundwater. The SDWA requires a program of regular testing of public water supplies and wells, and establishes drinking water standards to protect public health. However, regulations under the SDWA still do not require analysis for most of the synthetic organic compounds associated with hazardous waste sites, and there is no testing program for the domestic wells that serve some 40 million people in the United States.

Federal and state laws designed to protect groundwater have focused on chemical contamination from landfills and surface impoundments at industrial facilities. However, landfills and wastewater impoundments are not the only sources of groundwater contamination. Other industry-related sources include chemical leaks from storage areas, accidental spills, and vapor condensate from solvent recovery systems. Increasing regulation by local, state, and federal agencies has effectively barred the use of many traditional disposal facilities that were available to industry, leading to poor housekeeping and dependence on unsuitable sites within plant boundaries.

Non-industrial sources of groundwater pollutants in-

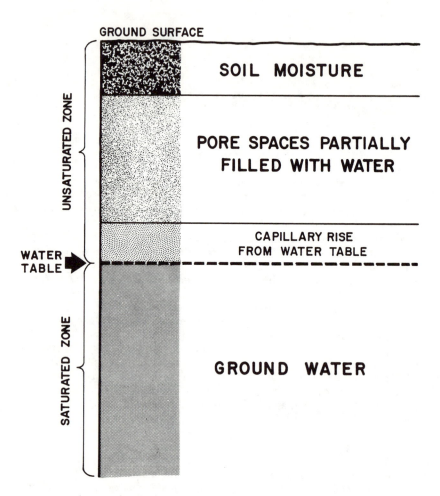

Figure 1.   Relationship between unsaturated and saturated zones (after Edward E. Johnson, Inc., 1966).

clude road runoff, municipal landfills, junkyards, and domestic waste water. Household products contain many soluble organic chemicals that find their way into septic
tanks, cesspools, and leaky sewer lines and from there migrate to the water table. In fact, some products used for
unclogging septic tank drain-fields contain industrial solvents suspected of being human carcinogens. Common commercial operations, such as automotive service, auto body re-
pair, dry cleaning, and printing are often unsuspected major contributors to local and regional groundwater contamination.

The lack of monitoring at tens of thousands of sites
where there is a potential for contamination, along with
the lack of comprehensive analysis of water quality at hundreds of thousands of wells, rules out the possibility for
a reliable determination of the extent and severity of
groundwater degradation and associated health risks in the
United States. In the absence of monitoring programs, segments of important aquifers have become degraded and may be
essentially lost forever as sources of drinking water.
Most important, portions of our population have been exposed to chemically contaminated drinking water for unknown
periods of time.

The nation's groundwater resource is huge. More than
one-third of the nation is underlain by aquifers capable of
yielding at least 100,000 gallons per day to an individual
well and at almost any location, groundwater can provide a
supply sufficient for single-family domestic use. Groundwater contamination is typically a local phenomenon, affecting only the uppermost aquifers. Contamination generally occurs in an area less than a mile long and a half-
mile wide, with pollutants moving at an average rate of
less than one foot per day.

Although the specific volume of contaminated groundwater may be only a very small percentage of the nation's
groundwater resource, the impact of this contamination can
be very large. There is a critical need to identify and
manage contamination sites both from the standpoint of protecting public health and preserving the resource.

Mechanisms Affecting Groundwater Contamination

Chemicals pass through several different hydrologic
zones (Figure 1) as they migrate through the soil to the
water table, the upper surface of the groundwater system.
The pore spaces in this region are occupied by both air and

GROUND WATER

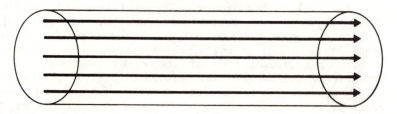

Figure 2A. Flow paths of molecules of water in laminar flow (Fetter, 1980).

SURFACE WATER

Figure 2B. Flow paths of molecules of water in turbulent flow (Fetter, 1980).

water (the unsaturated zone). Flow in this zone is vertically downward, as liquid contaminants or solutions of contaminants and precipitation move under the force of gravity.

The uppermost region of the unsaturated zone (the soil
zone) is the site of important processes leading to pollutant attenuation. Some chemicals are retained in this zone
by adsorption onto organic material and chemically active
silt and soil particles. These adsorbed chemicals can sub-
sequently be decomposed through oxidation and microbial activity. Many end-products are taken up by plants or released to the atmosphere.

Below the soil zone, the pore spaces are also unsaturated and as chemical-bearing precipitation percolates
through this zone, oxidation and aerobic biological degradation continue to take place. Some chemicals are also adsorbed in this zone and precipitates may be filtered out.

In the capillary zone, spaces between soil particles
may be saturated by water rising from the water table under
capillary forces. Certain chemicals which are lighter
than water will "float" on top of the water table in this
zone. These floating chemicals may move in different directions and at different rates than contaminants which
are dissolved in the percolating recharge.

Groundwater Flow

Once dissolved contaminants reach the water table,
they enter the groundwater flow system -- which is both
horizontal and vertical depending on the hydraulic gradients. All pore spaces between soil particles below the
water table are saturated. The relative unavailability of
dissolved oxygen in the saturated zone limits the potential
for oxidation of chemicals. Varying levels of attenuation
may take place, depending on the geologic conditions.

Unlike the turbulent flow of surface-water systems,
groundwater flow is laminar; particles of fluid move along
distinct and separate paths, with little mixing occurring
as the groundwater moves (Figure 2). Dissolved chemicals
in the saturated zone will flow with the groundwater. The
direction of flow is governed by hydraulic gradients and
groundwater will move in response to differences in hydro-
static head.

The major components of the flow system are the recharge area (where flow is generally downward) and the dis-

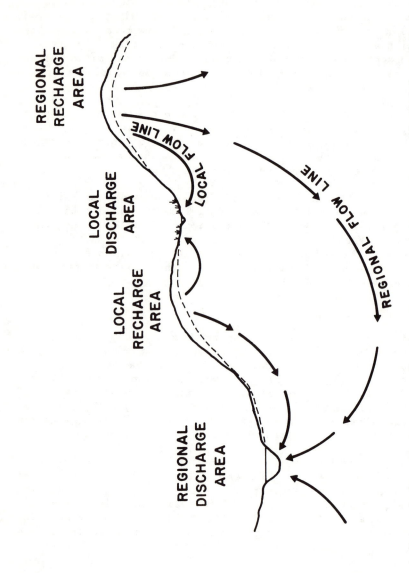

Figure 3. Groundwater flow pattern in a homogeneous isotropic aquifer with moderate relief.

charge area (where flow may be generally upward)(Figure 3).
The direction of flow in a shallow, local flow system could
in some cases be opposite to flow in a deeper flow system.
The ability of a monitoring well to detect the presence of
a plume is therefore based on the locations and depth at
which the well is set (Figure 4). Knowledge of the flow
system is an essential precondition in assessing chemical
contamination problems and a monitoring program implemented
without adequate hydrogeological information can be very
misleading.

Groundwater flow rates in aquifers generally range
from a few inches to a few feet per day. A body of contaminated groundwater may contain the accumulation of decades
of leachate discharge; and it may take many years for contaminants to be detected in a nearby water supply.

Plume Formation and Movement

Because groundwater flows in a laminar fashion, dissolved chemicals will follow groundwater flow lines and
form distinct plumes. Plumes of contaminated groundwater
have been traced from a few feet to several miles down-
stream of the pollution source.

The shape and size of a plume depends on a number of
factors including the local geologic framework, local and
regional groundwater flow, the type and concentration of
contaminants, and variations in the rates of leaching.
Figure 5 illustrates the shapes of two plumes of contamination in different geologic settings (basalt vs. sand and
gravel) and the lengths of time it took for them to develop.

The fact that chemicals are attenuated in the soil
through adsorption and chemical interaction with other organic and inorganic constituents of the aquifer makes it
difficult to predict the movement and fate of chemicals in
the groundwater. Volatile organic chemicals in groundwater
are extremely mobile. Other variables affecting mobility
are solubility, adsorption characteristics and degradation.
A schematic representative of the relative movement of
chemicals in groundwater is shown in Figure 6.

The density of contaminated fluids is another important factor in the formation and movement of a plume.
Lighter chemicals will tend to flow on top of the water
table, while the more dense will sink to the bottom. Differences in density of chemical pollutants have led to the
complex pattern of plumes illustrated in Figure 7. Note

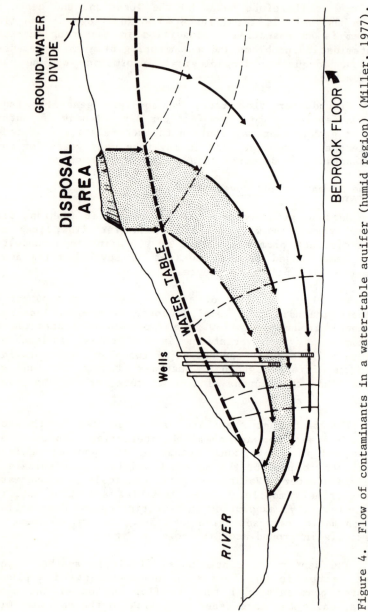

Figure 4. Flow of contaminants in a water-table aquifer (humid region) (Miller, 1977).

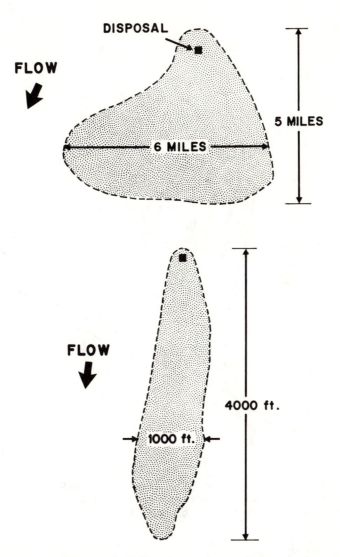

Figure 5. Effect of differences in geology on shapes of contamination plumes. (A) Chloride plume, Inel, Idaho. Aquifer: basalt. Time: 16 years. (B) Chromium plume, Long Island. Aquifer: sand and gravel. Time: 13 years.

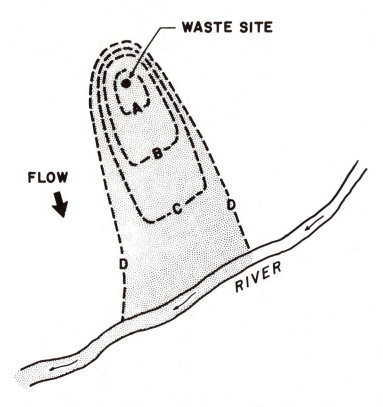

Figure 6.   Schematic diagram showing areal extent of contamination by different specific contaminants A, B, C, and D in
a mixed-waste plume in a water-table aquifer (after LeGrand,
1965).

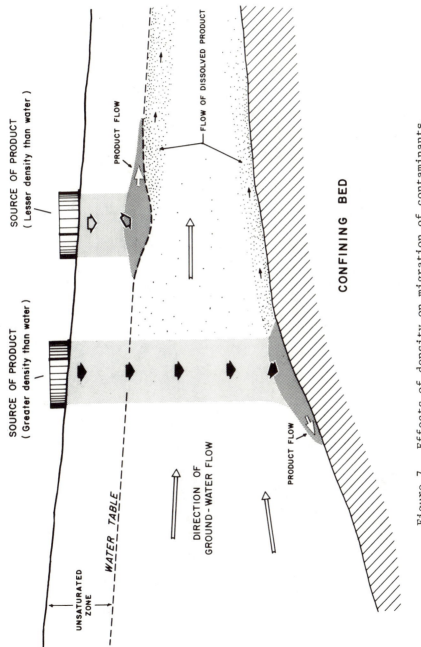

Figure 7. Effects of density on migration of contaminants.

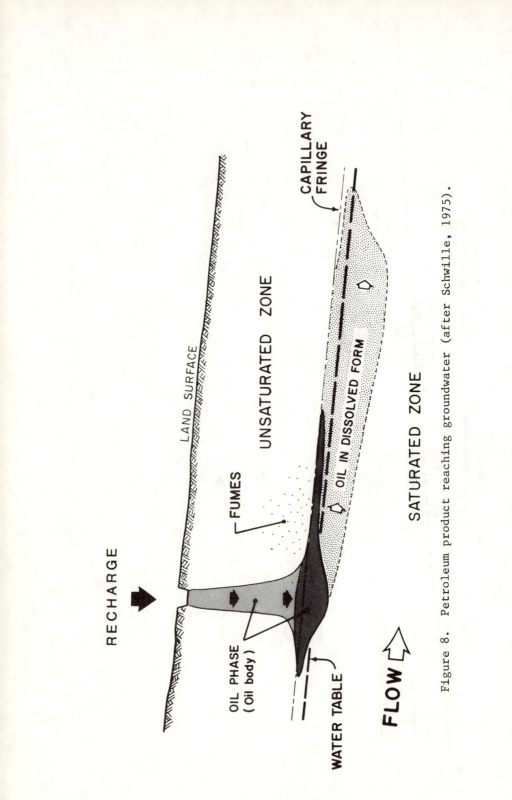

Figure 8. Petroleum product reaching groundwater (after Schwille, 1975).

that the figure shows a heavy product which is denser than water flowing down the slope of a confining bed in a direction which is opposite to the flow of the dissolved and floating product.

Slightly soluble materials may flow in multiple phases. For example, oil can move as a body, flowing on the surface of the groundwater table (Figure 8). It can also be dissolved, permeating the groundwater aquifer. In addition, the undissolved phase may give off vapors which migrate through the unsaturated zone in patterns which are unrelated to the groundwater flow system.

Surveys of groundwater contamination are further complicated by the variability of operating practices at typical waste disposal facilities. There can be numerous distinct plumes of contamination moving independently away from the site. Discontinuous discharges may result in "slugs" of contaminated water, causing wide spatial and temporal fluctuations in well-water quality (Figure 9). Lenses of sand and clay can cause other variations due to stratification of the contaminants. Pumping from wells can modify groundwater flow patterns and consequently alter the movement of a contaminant plume (Figure 10).

Furthermore, detailed monitoring of sites more than five years old has revealed fluctuations in the concentration of some constituents while other constituents remained relatively constant. This phenomenon is caused by the solution and dissolution of certain chemicals as the plume of contamination interacts with geologic materials in its path. Thus, the factors influencing movement of groundwater and contaminants within aquifers are complex, and the investigation of groundwater contamination can require extensive and costly work over a considerable time.

Groundwater Monitoring

Introduction

There are at least three spatial scales of groundwater monitoring commonly in use. The first type is typically employed at or near a specific potential source of contamination where the source is limited in area and can be uniquely identified geographically. This includes such sources as industrial discharges, industrial lagoons, landfills, and sewage treatment facility discharges. A second type is public or private supply wells which are monitored for reasons of safeguarding public health. For example, thousands of public water supply wells are analyzed per-

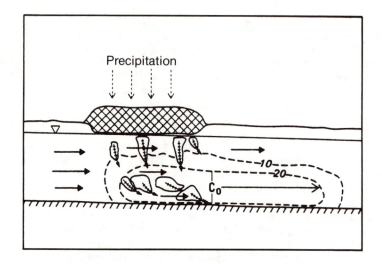

Explanation

⊤⊤⊤⊤⊤⊤⊤ **Hydrologic Boundary**

~~10~~ ~~20~~ **Line of Equal Dilution**—Number is dilution factor (see text section "Flow of Leachate")

C_0 ⟶ **Region of Approximately Uniform Concentration**—C_0 is initial concentration of leachate-enriched ground water at downgradient side of landfill

⟶ **Direction of Ground-Water Flow**

Leachate Pocket—Direction of flow and idealized shape of high-density leachate pocket

▽ **Water Table**

XXXXXXX **Landfill Deposits**

Figure 9. Leachate movement in groundwater beneath a landfill (Kimmel and Braids, 1980).

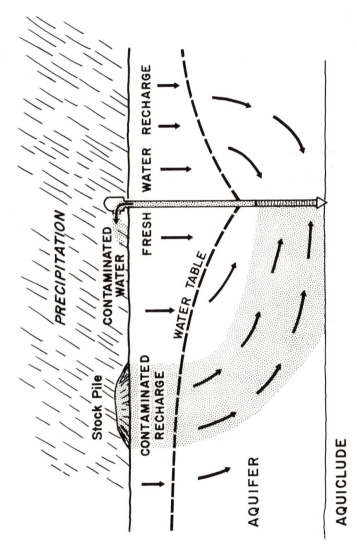

Figure 10.   Influence of pumping on plume migration (after Deutsch, 1963).

iodically for standard inorganic chemical constituents. This type of sampling is a form of quality control and is analogous to samples taken from the production line of a food processing plant for spot checking.

The third type of monitoring is a regional monitoring approach that is aimed at assessing the effects of diffuse sources and/or the combined effect of many point sources of contamination. Such diffuse sources include storm water runoff, on-lot septic systems, and the use of home fertilizers. This type of monitoring is particularly effective in suburban and urban locales with varied potential sources of groundwater pollution.

The major reason for installing monitoring wells is to provide early warning of groundwater contamination. If properly designed, monitoring networks can also aid in determining the effectiveness of engineered groundwater protection measures (such as impoundment liners) by providing information which may help protect disposal site operators against unjustifiable complaints, and in designing future disposal sites in comparable environments. The ultimate effectiveness of monitoring wells is dependent upon a clear definition of the desired results. For example, a monitoring program designed to supply information for litigation is quite different from one implemented to determine whether a liner is effectively sealing a landfill from an underlying aquifer. Monitoring based upon a regulatory philosophy of zero discharge to groundwater will require a monitoring system substantially different in design from one reflecting a regulatory philosophy of containment within the boundaries of the disposal site. Whatever the reason for installing a groundwater monitoring system, its design should be based on demonstrated hydrogeologic principles and site-specific data.

Hydrogeologic Investigation

Preliminary Survey. The first step in the hydrogeologic investigation of a site is the collection and review of soils, geologic, and groundwater resource reports, test boring data, well logs, well records, and water-quality data for the general vicinity of the disposal site. These data may indicate whether a site overlies an important aquifer, its depth, the general direction of flow, the ambient quality of water in the aquifer, and the presence of other water-bearing strata. In many cases an on-site inspection is also required to obtain additional detailed information.

Geophysical Surveys.   In some geohydrologic environments, one or more geophysical exploration methods may be
used in predesign data collection. Electrical earth resis-
tivity and seismic surveys, and specific conductance/tem-
perature studies can furnish supplemental information at
reasonable costs. However, data from any of these surveys
should be combined with drilling and sampling to confirm
findings.

Test Drilling.   A number of exploratory borings are
generally required before geologic, hydrologic, and geo-
chemical conditions can be defined. The number and depth
of these borings may vary depending on specific geohydrologic conditions and the size of the disposal area. Typical costs for determining groundwater quality at an industrial disposal site where contamination has occurred can
range from $25,000 to several hundred thousand dollars, de-
pending on the nature and extent of the work. An initial
effort may only determine the extent of contamination and
its rate of movement. The investigation may not provide
sufficient data to make a confident prediction of the future movement of the plume or concentrations of particular
chemicals. Such a detailed analysis may require thousands
of dollars more in field work, computer time, and special-
ized labor.

On relatively small sites, where the underlying earth
materials are fairly homogeneous, low in permeability, and
uniformly sloping in one direction, four to six borings extending to bedrock or a depth of 50 or so feet should suffice. Temporary wells tapping the uppermost water-bearing
section should provide sufficient data on the water-table
slope and background water quality to support initial conclusions concerning the nature and extent of contamination.
However, most geologic formations are not homogeneous, and
locally the flow paths of groundwater through them may be
considerably different from those of the region. If more
than one aquifer is present, each may have to be evaluated
with an appropriate number of properly spaced wells.

Design and Installation of Monitoring Well Networks

Under non-pumping conditions, the water-table config-
uration is generally a subdued replica of the land surface
topography. In this instance, monitoring wells should be
situated down the topographic slope from a disposal site,
between it and the nearest natural discharge point, such as
a stream or marshy area. However, when the cone of influence of a nearby pumping well extends beneath the site,

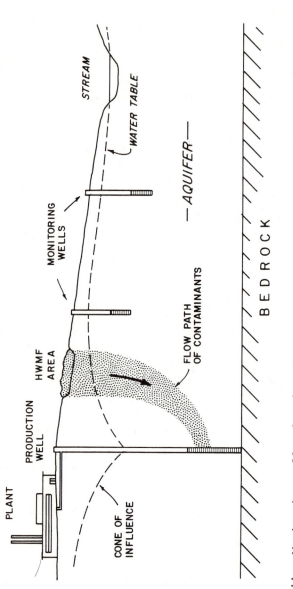

Figure 11. Monitoring wells placed at lower topographic elevations in the direction of natural groundwater flow may not be effective if contaminants are captured by the cone of influence of a nearby pumping well.

groundwater will flow toward that well preventing the detection of contamination in monitoring wells positioned according to topographic slope (Figure 11). In such cases, sampling the production wells might be all that is required to detect contamination from the disposal site.

Even when monitoring wells are properly located with respect to hydraulic gradients, groundwater contamination may not be detected unless the wells are screened in that portion of the aquifer through which contamination is traveling. For example, wells screened in the upper part of the zone of saturation may not detect contamination that moves downward and then through the lower portion of the aquifer to a discharge point (Figure 12). On the other hand, contaminants less dense than water may move only along the top of the zone of saturation, thereby evading detection in monitoring wells screened in a lower portion of the aquifer (Figure 13).

At disposal sites receiving mixed wastes, clusters of monitoring wells screened at different depths in the aquifer should be installed if optimum monitoring results are to be assured. A well cluster network is required if more than one aquifer is to be monitored.

Screening the entire section of earth materials penetrated by the borehole is an alternative method sometimes used in multi-aquifer locations (Figure 14). This type of installation yields a composite sample derived from all water-bearing strata penetrated. Some of these strata might contain only natural groundwater because the plume of contamination is traveling as a discrete body controlled by the flow system. In such cases, water samples collected from the well would be a composite mixture of groundwater. Because of this dilution, the sample would contain a low level of contamination but would indicate the presence of chemicals that are not found in water representing background conditions.

Monitoring wells drilled through, or finished in, waste fill areas to detect contamination may be effective only if a permanent watertight seal can be placed between the excavated hole and well casing. If improperly sealed, this zone provides a conduit for contamination to reach the aquifer more quickly than would be possible through undisturbed earth materials. In addition, improperly constructed monitoring wells can be an important source of cross-contamination between individual clean and dirty aquifers.

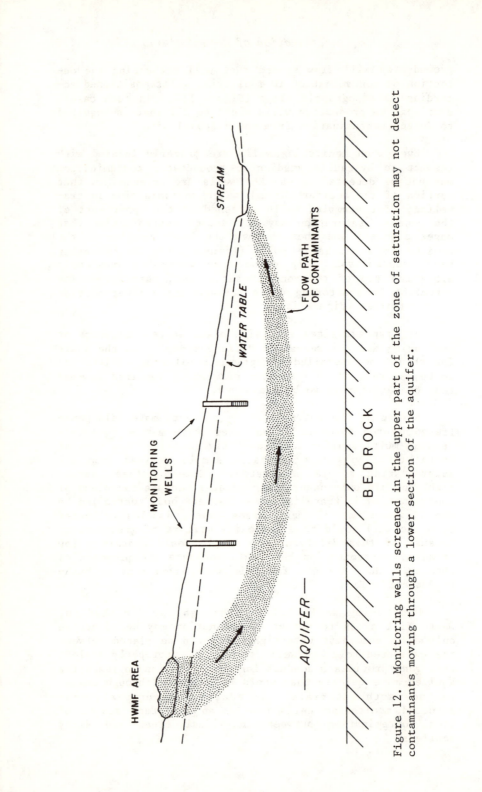

Figure 12. Monitoring wells screened in the upper part of the zone of saturation may not detect contaminants moving through a lower section of the aquifer.

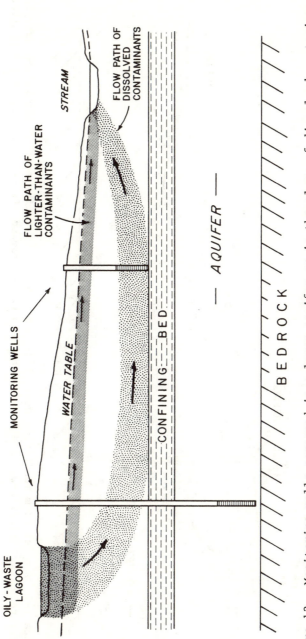

Figure 13. Monitoring wells screened in a lower aquifer or in the plume of dissolved contaminants may not detect lighter-than-water components of contamination.

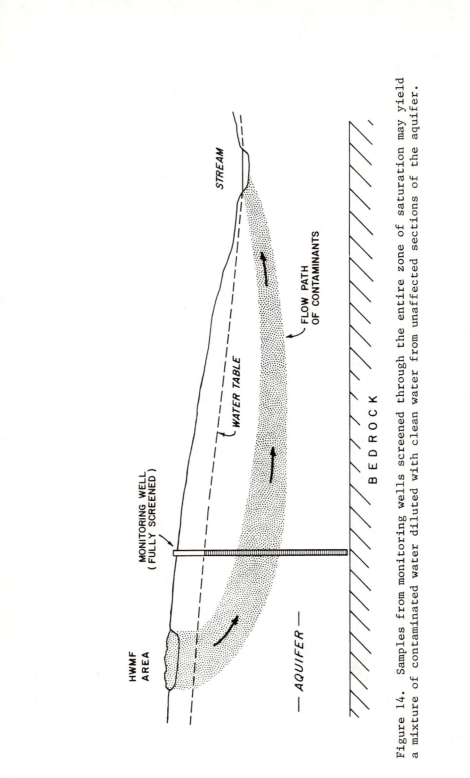

Figure 14. Samples from monitoring wells screened through the entire zone of saturation may yield a mixture of contaminated water diluted with clean water from unaffected sections of the aquifer.

Significant factors to consider when selecting and installing monitoring well casings include the kind of materials used, inside diameter, and wall thickness. Materials normally used are either metal or plastic. Interference with chemical analyses of groundwater samples may occur because of chemical reactions with the casing, pipe, cutting oils and threading compounds, cleaning solvents, or cement.

Sampling Monitoring Wells

Water samples may be collected from monitoring wells by a number of different types of pumps or bailers. Where the water table is within about 20 feet of land surface, shallow well suction pumps are commonly used for sampling. Airlift pumps and jet pumps may also be used to sample from shallow depths, as well as from depths beyond the suction limits of the shallow well pump. For pumping lifts greater than about 50 feet, deep well jet or submersible pumps usually prove to be the most practical means of sampling.

The equipment selected for sampling is dependent upon the type of chemicals of interest and their susceptibility to change due to aeration or agitation. Standing water in the casing should always be removed, and sampling protocol should be established for each well, recorded, and carefully followed during each sampling incident.

Several measurements may be made during sampling that provide useful data. Temperature should be taken as the water leaves the well. Specific conductance (related to total dissolved solids concentration), dissolved oxygen, and pH can be determined easily with portable battery-operated instruments. Dissolved oxygen is most accurately measured by passing a water stream over the probe in a container that prevents contact with the atmosphere.

Even properly developed monitoring wells may produce turbid or even muddy water. Ions adsorbed on silt, clay, and organic particles suspended in such samples may be placed in solution if certain preservatives are added directly to the sample. In the chemical analysis, this can result in higher concentrations of these ions which do not reflect the true water quality. Settling and filtration are the two primary field methods for reducing or eliminating suspended matter. The method(s) selected depends upon the particle size of the suspended matter and specific analyses indicated for the sample.

Immediate analysis of water samples is the ideal method of obtaining a truly representative quality of the wa-

ter. However, if the laboratory is distant from the well,
sample preservation is important to prevent alteration of
the chemical quality of the sample prior to analysis. During transit of water samples, changes in temperature and
exposure to the atmosphere can lead to changes in pH and
subsequent alteration of the original ionic balance of the
solution.

Volatilization of organics, oxidation of heavy metals,
and many other chemical and biological reactions can occur
which may ultimately affect the concentration of the constituents present at the time of analysis. Storage at low
temperature $(4^{\circ}C)$ is the preferred way to preserve samples.

Frequency of Sampling

There is no established procedure for determining frequency of sampling at a disposal site. Frequency can be
based on groundwater flow rates, statistical analyses of
historical variations in concentrations of selected chemical parameters, distance of the well from the source, geologic setting of the monitoring well in comparison to that
of the source, the characteristics of the soil and rock
formations potentially affected, and the depth to the water
table. Because of the generally slow movement of groundwater, with velocities normally ranging from less than 75
to 150 feet per year, a sampling frequency greater than
quarterly is rarely justified. However, more frequent analysis on a monthly or bimonthly basis may be necessary to
establish initial trends, especially if there are significant variations in key constituents with each sampling
event.

After this history has been defined and evaluated,
longer periods of time between samples can be used. Also,
simple indicators of change in water chemistry at the monitoring well locations, such as total dissolved solids and
chloride, can be measured on a monthly or bimonthly basis
with a more complete analysis conducted on an annual basis.
All wells may not require the same sampling schedule.
Wells tapping a deep artesian aquifer, for example, would
not be sampled as frequently as those screened in the water-table aquifer underlying the landfill site.

Summary

Investigating and monitoring groundwater contamination
incidents are highly complex activities, which must be ap-
proached on a site-specific basis. Although general guide-

lines have been established for studying groundwater conditions, designing monitoring well systems, drilling, and sampling, each case offers its own complications and requires careful planning and periodic review as the investigative and monitoring work proceeds. Otherwise, significant investments in technical help, subsurface investigations, and sample analysis may be wasted and the data obtained either misleading or inconclusive.

Abatement and Remedial Measures

Introduction

Restoration of a badly contaminated aquifer to drinking-water quality is seldom undertaken and rarely achieved. The majority of remedial efforts currently under way could be more accurately characterized as containment programs that result in only partial cleanup of the aquifer. They involve removal of the primary source of contamination such as a leaky lagoon, discarded drums, or body of spilled petroleum product. Geohydrologic investigations to determine the extent of contamination are then undertaken, followed in most cases by some action to monitor or limit the spread of the contaminated ground water.

The technology to remove some of the common groundwater contaminants is available today but is most cost-effectively applied at the water-supply wellhead. In view of the large volumes of water that would have to be pumped to remove and purify contaminated groundwater, complete restoration of the aquifer is in most cases not economically feasible.

Hydrogeologic investigations to define contamination problems can cost from $25,000 to $250,000. Litigation may lead to a doubling of this cost. The minimum cost of the groundwater phase of a partial cleanup and containment project is $500,000. Average costs for a typically complex plume of contaminated groundwater range from $5 to 10 million per site. The cost of total restoration of a badly contaminated aquifer to potable quality could be orders of magnitude greater, with time for completion measured in decades.

Present costs for treatment of public water supplies contaminated with organic contaminants range from $1.50 to $4.00 per month per family served. Research and development efforts to reduce costs of treatment can be expected to be stepped up in recognition of the high cost and difficulty of aquifer restoration.

Containment Techniques

A body of contaminated groundwater, or plume, can be contained in several ways. One approach is to impound the plume behind subsurface physical barriers. An alternative is to alter the groundwater flow system by hydraulic methods. In some cases a plume can be neutralized or immobilized in place by subsurface injection of chemical or biological agents.

Physical containment methods include construction of slurry walls, or cement-filled trenches, around the plume. Barrier walls can also be constructed by a vibrating beam method or injection of cement into the soil through small-diameter wells. To be effective, the barrier must be tied into an underlying bedrock or low permeability formation. The contaminated area must also be capped with clay or other impermeable material to limit infiltration or rainfall. Since no man-made or natural formation can be considered absolutely impermeable, some form of continuous low-level water withdrawal from within the impounded area may also be required.

Physical containment can be quite effective under ideal conditions, but its feasibility is severely reduced in hard-rock conditions or sites where the contamination extends below 100 feet. Initial costs are high, but operation and maintenance is minimal.

Wells and drains can be used to contain contaminated groundwater by altering the natural flow system. The general concept is to intercept the moving plume or draw contaminated water into recovery wells. The water can then be discharged off-site or re-injected on-site, with or without treatment. As long as operation of a properly-designed pumping system is continued, contamination can be effectively contained by this technique. Over the long term, a moderate level of aquifer rehabilitation can be achieved if contaminated water is discharged off-site or treated and re-injected on-site.

Costs of construction of hydraulic containment systems are less than physical containment systems. Operation and maintenance are high, particularly if treatment and disposal of large volumes of contaminated groundwater are involved. Also, the system must be operated perpetually.

Some contaminants can be immobilized or degraded in the ground by injection of chemical or biological substances. The injected substances must be waste-specific

and designed to digest, precipitate, or otherwise neutral-
ize contaminants. For example, some heavy metals can be
rendered insoluble by addition of alkalis or sulfides.
Natural microbial digestion of some organic contaminants
can be enhanced by injection of oxygen and nutrients.
These procedures are frequently suggested but eliminated
in many areas because of the difficulty in achieving uniform distribution and mixing of substances in the subsurface environment. In very few instances have these procedures been successfully employed to produce potable water.

In the sense of permanently eliminating the potential
for movement of a plume, total-containment is probably impossible. All installed subsurface walls and barriers will
eventually deteriorate and leak. Perpetual operation of a
pumping system, although feasible, would impose substantial
economic burdens on future generations. Finally, it must
be recognized that from a practical standpoint, some plumes
cannot be blocked, immobilized, pumped out, or excavated.
They will simply have to be left as they are, slowly moving
through groundwater systems. Monitoring of the rate and
direction of travel of such plumes will have to be relied
upon to provide the safeguards needed for protecting public
health and the environment.

Aquifer Restoration by Treatment

Under this concept the contaminated aquifer is restored through water treatment processes. Water is pumped
from the affected aquifer, treated, and then either recharged back to the aquifer or discharged. A significant
problem is to design a pumping well system that will capture only the contaminated water in the plume. A pumping
well draws from all directions. It mixes water from the
intercepted plume with clean water from other regions of
the aquifer. This factor alone can require pumping and
treatment of many times the volume of a plume before all
of the contaminants are removed. To complicate the problem
further, the movement of some contaminants is retarded by
the soil and some geologic formations are difficult to
pump because of their low permeability.

Even though the technology is available to eventually
capture all contaminants by a recovery well system, seldom
can the cost of this approach be supported by private or
public funds. Treatment for purposes other than use for
potable supply is, therefore, generally limited to situations where pumpage of contaminated water is required for
plume containment. In such cases, treatment levels are
selected to protect the surface water body or sewage treatment plant to which the pumped water is discharged.

Ground-Water Management

Over the past several decades the implementation of various public health and environmental laws has led to the use of the land as the ultimate waste assimilator. This has contributed to the protection and improvement of air quality and surface water resources at the expense of groundwater quality. Until recently, the cause and effect relationships between activities such as waste disposal on the land surface and groundwater contamination were not well understood. Even as knowledge in this area has advanced, fragmented approaches to groundwater management have led to conflicting uses of aquifers for waste receiving and water supply. It is rapidly becoming apparent that a comprehensive approach is required to manage and protect the groundwater resource.

In recognition of the ever-increasing threat to groundwater quality posed by present waste disposal and land use practices, EPA issued a proposed National Ground-Water Protection Strategy in 1980 (U.S. EPA, 1980). The strategy clearly defined the groundwater management dilemma that is, groundwater degradation is a nearly inevitable consequence of modern economic growth, land use and industrial development. In short, aquifer protection and growth are in many cases incompatible. The Strategy proposed that a rational program of groundwater management should provide for flexibility - allowing for necessary tradeoffs between groundwater protection and activities which are essential to economic development and protection of other valuable resources.

The basis for tradeoffs in groundwater protection lies in the fact that not all groundwaters are of equal value. As it naturally occurs, groundwater may be fresh or quite saline; aquifers range from sands and gravels yielding prolific water supplies to very tight clays and fractured bedrock with no practical yield. Some aquifers, or portions of aquifers, are degraded by human activities and cannot be restored or treated to a useable quality. The value of aquifers may vary from one place to another. In one part of the country an aquifer may constitute a sole source of drinking water supply, while the best use of a similar aquifer in another region may be the extraction of oil or mineral deposits. The key to solving the groundwater management problem is to be able to determine the best use of individual aquifers. This can guide land use, resource development and waste management decisions. High risk activities can be channeled into areas where the groundwater is not used for water supply, and maximum protection can be

Table 1. States with Groundwater Classification Systems

Connecticut	North Carolina
Florida	Vermont
Maryland	Virginia
New Jersey	Wyoming
New Mexico	Territory of Guam
New York	

Source: (Magnuson, 1981)

cost-effectively provided to important aquifers and their recharge areas. Funds for costly cleanup efforts can be directed to sites where critical water supplies are at risk.

The best present and future use of an aquifer is determined not only by its physical type but by the complex interrelationships of site-specific physical, chemical, social and economic factors. Where sufficient data on population, land use, water quality and hydrogeology are available, the uses of different aquifers can be determined on a formal basis. In fact, groundwater classification systems, designating the uses of aquifers and the levels of protection required to maintain these uses, have been successfully adopted by several states (see Table 1). However, determining the use of aquifers can be a complex and controversial undertaking. Technical and policy issues can obstruct objective decision-making.

Regional Case History

Long Island, New York, is underlain by a multi-aquifer system typical of the Atlantic Coastal Plain. A large amount of data on water quality and hydrogeology are available for this area. The shallow, water-table aquifer has become generally contaminated due to urbanization, industrialization and past agricultural activities. The primary water-supply aquifer is the confined Magothy aquifer. At first, it was believed that the Magothy was naturally protected from contamination due to its confined nature. It is now known that the Magothy is recharged by the glacial aquifer in central regions, and the downwards movement of contaminated water into the Magothy has been documented.

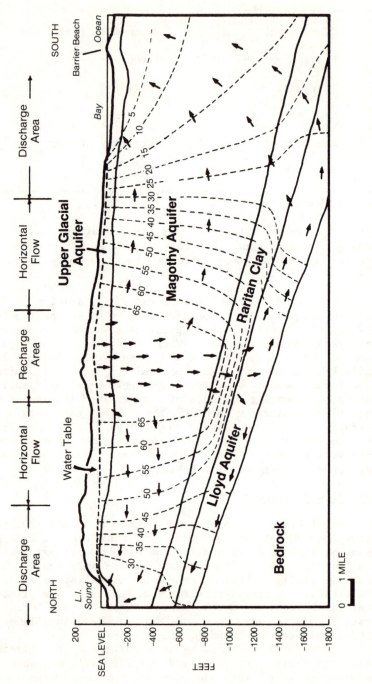

Figure 15. Three dimensional flow relationships in Nassau County, Long Island, New York.

Zones of recharge (downward flow), horizontal flow and discharge (upward flow) within the glacial aquifer have been identified and mapped (see Figure 15) to provide the basis for hydrogeologic zoning (Cohen et al., 1968).

Land use and water quality data were then taken into consideration to delineate eight hydrogeologic zones (see Figure 16) in the glacial aquifer. Wastewater management, pumpage and land use controls for each zone were developed (Nassau-Suffolk Regional Planning Board, 1978).

Zones I and III are deep recharge zones without significant conflicting land uses. The use of the shallow aquifer within these zones is to recharge the Magothy aquifer. Public land acquisition and low density residential development are recommended in these zones for aquifer protection. Zone II is a heavily industrialized zone within the recharge zone. This area is so heavily contaminated that is essentially "written-off" as a drinking-water supply. Industrial pumpage is encouraged in this zone to help recirculate and contain the contaminated water. Zone VIII is a discharge zone which is adjacent to a surface water body that is not very sensitive to groundwater discharge quality. This zone is recommended for future landfill siting.

Although the Long Island hydrogeologic zoning system has not been formally adopted by the state of New York, it is being implemented at many levels of government. The state agencies use it as a guide for landfill siting and in detemining sewer needs in the construction grants program under the Clean Water Act. County health agencies limit septic system densities based on the plan, and local governments have adopted zoning ordinances to protect recharge areas. The New York State Legislature is considering the purchase of 100,000 acres in the Zone III recharge area for the purpose of aquifer protection.

Local Case Study

This case study involves the contamination of a water supply well serving a small community. It illustrates how failure to protect critical aquifers through land use planning can severely limit a town's options when confronted with a contamination problem. Further, it illustrates the sensitivity of a supply well to relatively small contamination sources, and highlights the need for stringent measures to protect aquifers from nonpoint sources of contamination.

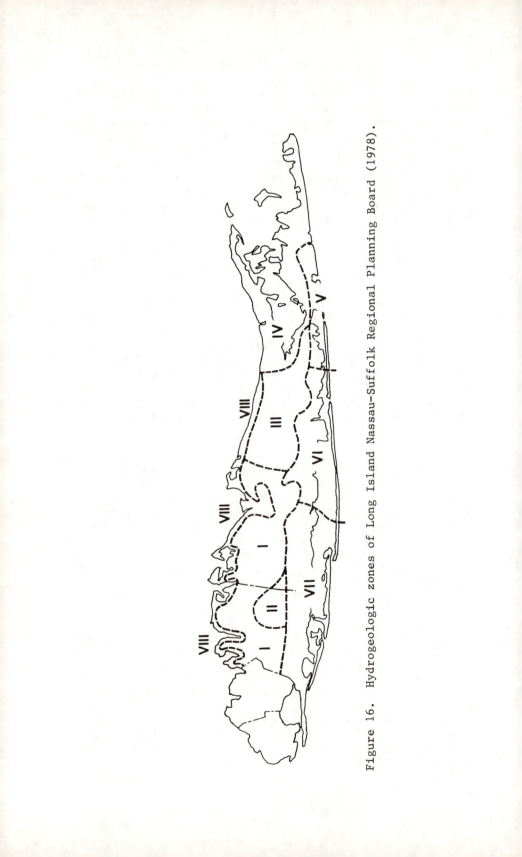

Figure 16. Hydrogeologic zones of Long Island Nassau-Suffolk Regional Planning Board (1978).

In 1979, when utilities first began to sample their wells for organic chemicals, it was discovered that one of this community's wells yielded water containing several hundred parts per billion of an industrial solvent. Drilled in the early 1950's, the well represented about half of the safe yield of the water supply system. Since there were no federal guidelines for these compounds, the state health department set an arbitrary limit of 20 parts per billion and required that the utility take the well out of service.

An investigation of possible sources of contamination was carried out and a small electronics industry was identified approximately 1,000 feet upgradient of the well. From its location, any contaminant that might be discharged or spilled would eventually flow through the aquifer system into the public supply well.

Through a detailed hydrogeologic study it was determined that the plume of contamination was approximately 1,000 feet long, 200 feet wide and 75 feet thick. It was estimated to contain nearly 50 million gallons of contaminated groundwater. Calculations revealed that less than 20 gallons of industrial solvent spilled at the site or leached from the soil over time could have created this plume.

Because the lost water supply well represented a major portion of the community supply, the utility immediately investigated ways to eliminate the contamination or to develop new groundwater sources. The first alternative evaluated was treatment at the wellhead. However, it was found that this would involve an investment of over one million dollars which was beyond the resources of the utility at that time. The second alternative was to replace the water supply well with a new well in another aquifer area.

An investigation of groundwater conditions within the franchise area identified three sites where the one million gallon per day pumpage could be supported. Figure 17 shows the location of the contaminated supply and the areas of maximum groundwater potential which were investigated. Unfortunately, all three of these sites were ruled out because of existing adverse land uses. At the most promising site there is a hazardous waste disposal facility. Any new pumpage in this area might draw contaminants into the well. The second site had been developed as a residential area with on-lot septic systems. Such areas have been ruled out for water supply purposes by the state health department. The third area was located in a state park. Groundwater

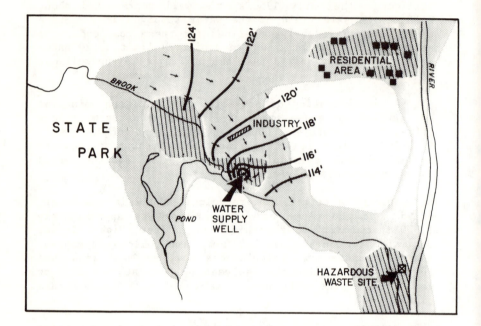

—————— 120'   Water-table contour (feet above mean sea level)

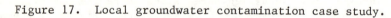   Direction of groundwater flow

▓▓▓▓▓   Extent of buried valley aquifer

\\\\\\\\\\   Area of maximum groundwater pumpage potential

Figure 17.   Local groundwater contamination case study.

development by a private utility is not one of the accepted
uses of park land. The development of an alternative supply was therefore preempted in all three sites.

The utility then conducted additional groundwater investigations in the vicinity of the affected water supply
well. The results indicated that the contaminated well
could be used to intercept contaminants and prevent their
reaching a new supply well to be drilled a few hundred feet
away. This alternative was selected. The old well was
pumped at 1/2 million gallons per day, and discharged to a
sewer, thus acting as a barrier to migrating contaminants.
The new well was placed on line and pumped at 1/2 million
gallons per day.

The new well and barrier well have been in operation
for more than four years. Through this period the community has lived under emergency water use restrictions because of the reduced yield of the system. Although low
levels of organic chemicals have occasionally been present
in the new supply well, the barrier well has successfully
protected it for use as a public supply. The industry,
although not admitting guilt, has taken steps to eliminate
the source. It has improved its solvent handling and storage practices to avoid spills and leaks, and has excavated
and removed sludges containing organic chemicals that had
been buried on site. In addition, it installed an inter-
ceptor well on its own property to pump and contain the
heavily contaminated groundwater which was found to underlie the plant site. This water is treated and then discharged to the local sanitary sewer.

The cleanup activities have resulted in a marked reduction in the concentration of organic chemicals in the
original supply well. Because of the slow movement of
groundwater and the 1,000-foot distance from the source
of contamination to the well, it took nearly a year for
cleanup activities at the plant facility to be reflected
in well quality. The concentration of organic chemicals
now averages about 20 parts per billion, compared to the
original 200 parts per billion. The utility is now seeking permanent solutions which will enable it to place the
well back in service.

The lessons to be learned from this case study center
on ways in which this costly contamination problem could
have been avoided. If the town had performed an inventory
of critical aquifer areas and adopted special groundwater
protection zoning districts it could have protected two of
the three alternative aquifer areas for use as supple-

mentary well fields.   Zoning in these areas should have
called for low density residential housing development and
prohibited industrial uses and waste disposal.   Parcels
large enough to serve as well fields (i.e. 10-15 acres)
could have been purchased to assure development of new
well sites in one or more of these areas.

In addition, the utility, with the support of the community health enforcement agent, should have performed an
inventory of activities, especially industrial activities
upgradient of the well site to identify poor housekeeping
practices (i.e. storage of unprotected materials outdoors,
disposal of wastes on site, and high potential for spills
during materials handling with no visible means of spill
control) which might threaten groundwater quality.   To prevent or correct such activities, the community could have
adopted special health regulations governing non-residen-
tial uses which would require good housekeeping practices
to be employed.

Another lesson to be learned from this case study is
the sensitivity of the aquifer to a relatively small source
of pollution discharged from what was originally perceived
as a clean industry.   Less than a gallon per week of material leaked or accidentally discharged from the site was
probably responsible for shutting down a one million gallon
per day well.

Finally, it should be noted that this well contamination incident was not caused by a major hazardous waste
landfill or lagoon.   In this respect, it is by no means
unique.   Land-use related non-point sources can be significant contributors to groundwater contamination problems.
In most cases these sources can only be controlled at the
local level.   It is up to the cities and towns, encouraged
and assisted by the state and federal governments, to identify critical aquifers and adopt land use and health controls which will effectively prevent contamination of
existing and future water supplies.

Conclusion

The complex nature of the hydrogeologic system renders
the evaluation of contaminant migration in the ground a
difficult task.   To be successful, a hydrogeologic investigation must have a clearly defined objective.   The accurate
definition of the flow system is critical to the success of
the study and must take into consideration a wide range of
natural and artificial influences.   Sampling techniques

must be chosen to suit the site conditions and protocols carefully executed.

Through the completion of properly designed investigations on the local and regional scale the real nature and extent of the nation's groundwater problem will be known. Only then will government and industry be in a position to design and select cost-effective approaches to aquifer cleanup.

The most effective means to guarantee the long-term availability of groundwater resources is the development and implementation of programs to protect aquifers from land use activities that degrade water quality. Land acquisition and land use controls in critical recharge areas are examples of essential components of aquifer protection.

References

Braids, O.C., G.R. Wilson, and D.W. Miller, "Effects of Industrial Waste Disposal on the Ground-Water Resource," Drinking Water Quality Enhancement Through Source Protection. Ann Arbor Science Publishers Inc. 1977.

Cohen, Philip, Franke, O.L., and Foxworthy, B.L., 1968. An Atlas of Long Island's Water Resources. New York State Water Resources Commission Bulletin 62., Albany, New York.

Deutsch, M., "Groundwater Contamination and Legal Controls in Michigan." U.S. Geological Survey Water-Supply Paper 1691. 1963.

Edward E. Johnson Inc., Ground Water and Wells. St. Paul, Minnesota. 1966.

Fetter Jr., C.W., Applied Hydrogeology. Charles E. Merrill Publishing Company, Columbus, Ohio. 1980.

Kimmel, G.E., and O.C. Braids, "Leachate Plumes in Ground Water From Babylon and Islip Landfills, Long Island, New York." U.S. Geological Survey Professional Paper 1085. 1980.

LeGrand, H.E., "Patterns of Contaminated Zones of Water in the Ground." Water Resources Research, Vol. 1, pp. 83-95. 1965.

Magnuson, Paula L., 1981. Groundwater Classification. Draft contract report prepared for the U.S. Environmental Protection Agency, Office of Drinking Water. Copyright 1982 by Geraghty & Miller, Inc., Syosset, N.Y.

Magnuson, Paula L., 1982. Groundwater Classification Paper presented at the Sixth National Groundwater Quality Symposium, Atlanta, Georgia.

Miller, D.W., editor, <u>The Report to Congress on Waste Disposal Practices and Their Effects on Drinking Water.</u> Office of Water Supply and Office of Solid Waste Management Program, U.S. Environmental Protection Agency. January 1977.

Miller, D.W., F.A. DeLuca, and T.L. Tessier, "Ground-Water Contamination in the Northeast States." EPA-660/2-74-056. June 1974.

Nassau-Suffolk Regional Planning Board. 1978. The Long Island Comprehensive Waste Treatment Management Plan. Volume I. Summary Plan. Section 3.2.1. The Hydrogeologic Zones. Hauppauge, New York.

Schmidt, K.D., "Water Quality Variations for Pumping Wells." <u>Ground Water</u>, Vol. 5, No. 2, pp. 130-137. March-April 1977.

Schwille, F., "Groundwater Pollution by Mineral Oil Products." Proceedings of the Moscow Symposium. IAHS-Publication No. 103. 1975.

U.S. Environmental Protection Agency. 1980. Proposed Ground Water Protection Strategy. Office of Drinking Water. Washington, D.C.

5. Groundwater Protection Strategies: Federal, State and Local Relationships

Introduction

This country has witnessed a burgeoning interest in groundwater protection in recent years. Activity relating to development of groundwater protection strategies has escalated at the federal, state, and local levels. However, to date, no comprehensive national program exists for the protection of groundwater quality. This chapter reviews existing federal legislation dealing with groundwater protection; discusses the rationale for establishing a national groundwater protection policy; and proposes a framework for analyzing groundwater quality issues which defines appropriate federal, state, and local institutional relationships.

Existing Federal Legislation

Throughout the 1970´s, Congress enacted several laws addressing atmospheric and surface water pollution. Although several of these laws address segments of the groundwater pollution problem, no comprehensive national program has been established to systematically regulate groundwater quality. This section addresses existing federal legislation as it relates to groundwater protection.

Clean Water Act

The first major federal legislation potentially affecting groundwater quality was the Clean Water Act, 33 U.S.C. Section 1251, et seq. (1972). This Act regulates discharges of pollutants from point and nonpoint sources and provides for establishment of ambient standards for preventing the degradation of surface water quality. Although the term ˝groundwater˝ appears in the Clean Water Act, the U.S. Environmental Protection Agency (EPA) has construed the Act as primarily a surface water pollution control statute (Tripp and Jaffe, 1979).

The courts have been divided as to whether the Clean Water Act's permitting program under Section 402, U.S.C. Section 1342, was intended to regulate discharges to groundwater, but in any case have certainly not interpreted it as a broad mandate to protect groundwater. Section 208 of the Clean Water Act, 33 U.S.C. Section 1288, refers to groundwater, and some 208 plans, such as the Long Island water quality management 208 program, focused on groundwater quality protection strategies (LIRB, 1978).

Safe Drinking Water Act

The Safe Drinking Water Act (SDWA) of 1974, 42 U.S.C. Section 300f et seq. provides for development of primary and secondary ambient drinking water standards for the protection of human health. Primary standards establish maximum contaminant levels for ten inorganic and six organic chemicals, radionuclides, microbiological contaminants, and turbidity. Secondary standards deal with the odor and appearance of water and are not federally enforcible, but rather serve as guidelines for state programs. The SDWA also establishes deep well injection control and the sole source aquifer protection programs. Deep well injection control is aimed at controlling underground injection of industrial or municipal waste through wells into deep underground aquifers. The sole source aquifer protection program is designed to protect aquifers which are the sole or principal source of drinking water for an area, and which, if contaminated, would create a significant public health hazard.

Resource Conservation and Recovery Act

The Resource Conservation and Recovery Act of 1976 (RCRA), 42 U.S.C. Section 6901 et seq., includes solid waste disposal and hazardous waste facility regulatory programs. The act provides for regulation of hazardous wastes from their point of generation to disposal. Factors considered when classifying a solid waste as hazardous include: corrosiveness, ignitability, reactivity, or toxicity. Also included as hazardous are any wastes which pose a potential hazard to human health or the environment when improperly treated, stored, transported, disposed of, or otherwise managed. The Act authorizes EPA to require proper record keeping and labeling practices and the use of a manifest system to assure that hazardous wastes are designated for proper treatment, storage, and disposal. Implementation of the regulations promulgated under RCRA is the responsibility of the individual states.

Toxic Substances Control Act

The Toxic Substances Control Act of 1976 (TOSCA), 15 U.S.C. Section 2601 et seq. authorizes EPA to regulate toxic pollutants throughout their manufacture, processing, distribution, consumption, and disposal cycles. EPA is authorized by TOSCA to require the testing of chemical substances manufactured or processed by a company. Adverse information must be immediately reported by the company to EPA. EPA is allowed to regulate and ban, if necessary, any chemicals on the basis of unreasonable risk to human health or the environment.

Surface Mining Control and Reclamation Act

The Surface Mining Control and Reclamation Act of 1977, 30 U.S.C. Section 1201 et seq. (1978) requires operating permits, mining and reclamation plans, and permit approval procedures which explicitly recognize the potential impacts of surface mining on groundwater quality.

Superfund

The Comprehensive Environmental Response Compensation and Liability Act (CERCLA) of 1980 (Superfund), 42 U.S.C. Section 9605 et seq. grants the federal government authority to respond to releases or threatened environmental releases (without regard to whether releases are to surface water, groundwater, land, or air) of hazardous substances, and certain other pollutants that present an imminent danger to public health and welfare. An important distinction between CERCLA and the Clean Water Act is that the former holds certain generators and transporters of hazardous waste liable, as well as the owners and operators. Under the Clean Water Act, a generator is not liable for releases from an off-site storage facility controlled by an independent third party, unless the generator breached a reasonable standard of care (Evans and Frost, 1982). CERCLA makes responsible parties legally liable for response and cleanup costs whenever a hazardous substance is released.

Public Nuisance Legal Actions

The traditional common law of nuisance arose in England prior to nineteenth century industrialization and was used to obtain relief or compensatory damages from what today would be considered air or water pollution. In successful cases, the source of noxious odors, fumes, or effluents was typically situated close to the offended party so that the cause of the pollution was apparent, and the relief sought (often, to close the offending plant) would clearly achieve the goal of the legal action. The common law of nuisance, however, has seldom, if ever, been utilized to rectify a groundwater pollution problem. For a discussion of private and public nuisance laws see Prosser et al. (1976), Harper and James (1956), and Tripp (1976).

The U.S. Supreme Court may have greatly diminished the scope of federal common law as it applies to groundwater pollution. In The City of Milwaukee v. Illinois, 451 U.S. 304 (1981), the Supreme Court has effectively eliminated the federal common law remedy for pollution in situations where Congress has previously established statutory standards and procedures. In the City of Milwaukee case, the Supreme Court found that the Congress had already established standards in the Clean Water Act for controlling surface water pollution and that, therefore, no federal common law remedy was available. It is reasonable to assume that the federal court's treatment of groundwater pollution cases based on common law would be similar to that of surface water pollution. Of course, the City of Milwaukee decision does not foreclose state nuisance law remedies.

While the programs which these laws establish affect groundwater, none is a groundwater quality statute in the sense that the Clean Water Act is a surface water quality statute. None sets out a comprehensive groundwater quality strategy or policy; none establishes a national groundwater quality objective or process for establishing what the objective should be; none purports to address systematically the causes of groundwater pollution (Tripp and Jaffe, 1979). We have, therefore, gone through the 1970's without development of a comprehensive national program for addressing groundwater quality.

Rationale for a National
Groundwater Protection Strategy

On a conceptual basis, it is useful to identify those factors which support a national groundwater protection legal framework. In general, these factors justify a more comprehensive groundwater protection policy and programs for implementing that policy than exist today even though this is a political era where the federal government is embroiled in a major effort to reduce federal regulation.

Justification for Federal Involvement

First, groundwater is recognized as an increasingly important national resource for water supply, irrigation, and maintenance of aquatic and estuarine ecosystems. Therefore, the quality of this resource is ipso facto a matter of national concern.

Second, the groundwater pollution problem in this country is universal and ubiquitous. It is found in all parts of the country (EPA, 1977; Tripp and Jaffe, 1979; CEQ, 1981; Devine and Ballard, 1982; OTA, 1983). Although most groundwater may not flow across interstate boundaries and therefore affect interstate commerce directly, some does (e.g., the Ogallala Aquifer), and much groundwater is discharged into surface waters which move across interstate boundaries. Therefore, polluted groundwater in one state can indirectly affect the quality of water in another state. Such an interstate impact is a traditional reason given for federal action.

It is argued that since land use policies are the province of local or state governments and groundwater pollution arises from inappropriate land uses, the federal role must be limited. However, local governmental units have traditionally abdicated their role in the siting of hazardous waste disposal sites. The location of these sites is much more a reflection of indifference or susceptibility to economic pressure. Moreover, patterns of growth in developing areas are often more strongly influenced by federal infrastructure investment programs than by local planning. Infrastructure siting decisions and their attendant waste disposal problems have typically not arisen from deliberate land use choices of local units of government.

Third, the groundwater pollutants of increasing concern, namely, manmade toxic organic chemicals, are much more difficult to identify and control than so-called conventional pollutants. The scientific expertise available to deal with toxic contaminants in groundwater is much more limited than it was for traditional surface water contaminants (e.g., bacteria, suspended solids, or biological oxygen demand). The number of qualified groundwater hydrogeologists in the country is also rather small. Therefore, few local or state governments will be able to retain the requisite number of experts to develop groundwater quality management programs. A substantial federal role in groundwater quality management could help overcome this shortage of expertise.

Federal Ambivalence

Unfortunately, recognition of the national characteristics of groundwater quality protection and pollution control has come to the fore of national consciousness in the late 1970's and early 1980's, a time when political whims in terms of attitudes towards federalism are moving in the opposite direction. Since Congress expressed ambivalence about the federal role in management of the quality of groundwater resources throughout the 1970's, what will Congress do in the 1980's when the proverbial wisdom is that local units of government and states are more adept at maintaining environmental quality? The absence of federal guidance has created a dilemma for any effort to establish clear groundwater quality policies, strategies, and objectives.

Nevertheless, in 1982, EPA did take limited action in response to increasing political concern regarding abandoned industrial landfills and existing hazardous waste sites. On July 16, 1982, 47 Federal Register 31180 (Friday, July 16, 1982) (to be codified in 40 CFR Part 300), EPA promulgated the Superfund National Contingency Plan which is intended to prioritize abandoned hazardous waste landfills for Superfund cleanup. However, this plan failed to establish satisfactory criteria for landfill clean-up and is, as a consequence, being challenged by the Environmental Defense Fund (EDF).[1] On July 26, 1982, EPA promulgated the RCRA regulations for existing and new land disposal facilities as interim final rules, 47 Federal Register 32274 (Monday, July 26, 1982). Because these regulations fail to require preventive containment systems for existing hazardous waste facilities, they too are being challenged.[2] On December 20, 1982, EPA announced its proposed nationwide list of 418 toxic-waste sites eligible for Superfund financing.[3] EPA has also completed a draft of a

---

1. EDF v. EPA, No. 82-2234 (D.C. Cir. 1982). The complaint charges that EPA failed to incorporate appropriate health and environmental standards in the Plan and failed to provide opportunities for public participation in the Plan's preparation.

2. In Re Consolidated Land Disposal Regulation Litigation, No. 82-2205 and consolidated cases, including EDF v. Gorsuch, (D.C. Cir. 1982). These cases challenge, among other things, EPA's failure to require preventive containment systems, i.e., liners and leachate collection systems, for existing hazardous waste facilities.

surface impoundment report on the nation's municipal and industrial waste disposal sites.

Given prevailing attitudes by the Reagan Administration about federal, state, and local government relationships, in conjunction with EPA's budget and environmental regulation, the fact that EPA has taken these steps is a reflection of the political strength of the factors identified above which promote a national program for controlling groundwater pollution.

Cost-Benefit Considerations

An economic evaluation of groundwater pollution control programs is particularly complex, and any such analysis must be cognizant of the peculiar characteristics of groundwater. One characteristic is the practical irreversibility of groundwater pollution, causing the cost of clean-up to become prohibitively high irrespective of what the benefits may be. Another characteristic of groundwater is the typical slow, confined movement of groundwater and its contaminants. If we discount future values to estimate their present worth, we may conclude that there is little benefit in cleaning up polluted groundwater, leaving it to future generations to worry about. Yet, because groundwater pollution plumes do typically move slowly and are relatively confined, it is often possible to take measures to maintain the quality of the remainder of the affected groundwater resource. The whole subject of cost-benefit analysis relating to groundwater quality is further complicated by the fact that scientific knowledge about toxics, their movement through unsaturated and saturated soils, suitable monitoring formats, and health and ecological effects of toxic substances is inadequate.

Although restoring the quality of polluted groundwater may be an exceedingly complex and costly affair, it is a questionable ethical practice to impose the potential risks associated with groundwater contamination on future generations when steps can be taken today to prevent further contamination. Present generations are bearing the costs of Love Canal and an increasing number of polluted water supply wells resulting from industrialization, the direct benefits of which accrued to society decades ago.

------

3. U.S. Environmental Protection Agency Environmental News Region 6 (Dec. 20, 1982); New York Times, p. B13 (Wednesday, December 22, 1982).

A prerequisite for a site cleanup under a court injunction or CERCLA mandate is evidence of "imminent and substantial endangerment to public health or the environment." The legal assessment of such an endangerment requires the traditional "balancing of the equities" test inherent in any court ordered relief. The balancing of the equities necessitates cost-benefit considerations. The court must balance the cost to the defendant against the nature of the anticipated harm to be abated by the contemplated relief (Mott, 1982).

Case Study

Cost-benefit analysis played a critical role in the case study of the Cordova Chemical Company site in Dalton Township, Michigan, and may represent a pivotal precedent for future CERCLA remedial action (Mott, 1982). The Cordova site was among the first 17 "pre-Superfund" cleanup sites selected and was the site of a groundwater contamination problem resulting from previous waste disposal practices. Prior to CERCLA investigation, the Cordova Chemical Company had cooperated with state and local officials to clean up the waste disposal site and aid in the installation of an alternate drinking water supply. It was estimated that aquifer restoration would cost between $25-38 million without reclaiming the aquifer for drinking water use. Natural recovery of the aquifer was estimated to occur within 15-44 years without any remedial action.

Subsequent application of a cost-benefit analysis led to an informal decision by the EPA that remedial efforts to clean the groundwater aquifer would not be cost-effective (Mott, 1982). It was decided that scarce resources should not be devoted to a remedial program that had nominal environmental benefits and no benefits to public health.

Groundwater Quality Management Programs

The benefits of any groundwater protection program depend on the perceived long-term value of a particular groundwater resource to present and future generations. Any analysis of societal benefits and costs of different groundwater protection strategies must recognize that aquifers or aquifer segments have varying uses and levels of quality and, therefore, different values.

Aquifer Classification

To provide some degree of conceptual simplicity for a groundwater protection strategy, it is useful to define three classes of groundwater quality. One class would include aquifers or aquifer segments containing pristine high quality groundwater, the recharge watershed areas of which are largely undeveloped with few or no major sources of pollution. Strict land use controls within that recharge area provide the long-term prospect of maintaining the high quality of that system at low public cost. A second class includes the large majority of aquifers where some development in their recharge areas has occurred but the water is still of a quality suitable for potable use with reasonable treatment. A third class consists of those aquifers where, because of existing pollution or relative hydrologic isolation (minimizing the likelihood of migration of contaminants to unpolluted groundwater), the long-term costs of incremental degradation would not be severe.

Site Selection

This analysis suggests that the planning of hazardous waste facilities or deep wells for toxic waste injection must consider siting to be at least as important a criterion as the engineering design of the facility itself. Under the best of circumstances, hazardous waste facilities or injection wells may experience operational problems. They should, therefore, not be sited where the resulting pollution entails significant potential damage. Potential damage minimization or avoidance means that site selection for prospective hazardous waste facilities should be based on hydrogeologic as well as other land use factors, and potential sites should be limited to the recharge areas of the third class of aquifers -- those aquifers that are already polluted and/or hydrologically isolated, thereby providing maximum potential for containment of wastes. Those facilities should not be sited in the recharge watershed areas of either pristine aquifers or drinking water aquifers. Currently, exclusive focus within RCRA and SDWA regulatory programs on facility or well design neglects the importance of siting criteria.

Non-point Sources

In addition, for pristine aquifer systems, the management program must include deliberate land use controls on so-called non-point sources of groundwater pollution. These sources include large numbers of residential subsurface disposal systems, parking lots, highways, and lawn or agricultural fertilizer and pesticide application. Also included in a comprehensive management program must be prohibition of new major sources of toxic pollution in recharge watershed areas and curtailment of use of existing major sources of pollution.

This groundwater classification approach facilitates the identification of appropriate groundwater quality objectives and provides a framework for implementing national regulatory programs. This conceptual framework emphasizes the role of hydrogeologic factors in siting decisions and land use controls in establishing both clean-up priorities and preventing degradation of high quality groundwater. It should help to minimize overall societal costs and maximize benefits associated with use and enjoyment of groundwater resources.

Such a process means that local governments will necessarily have a critical role in groundwater quality management. In American society, the task of establishing land use controls on residential, commercial, or industrial uses or infrastructure facilities typically falls to local or regional units of government or the states. Utilization of land use controls by local or state governments in recharge areas to accomplish groundwater quality management objectives may face "taking" challenges based on the Fifth and Fourteenth Amendments to the U.S. Constitution. A federal framework which establishes a process for classifying groundwater, identifying recharge areas, and prescribing land use controls based on recharge watershed conditions can both promote such local and state initiatives and make them scientifically justifiable and legally defensible from challenges based on taking or other claims.

Case Studies of Land Use Control Programs

Local, county, or state governments which institute critical recharge watershed land use control programs inevitably must consider and often confront legal challenges based on arbitrary regulatory action and taking of property. Recent cases address the extent to which local government may reasonably impose controls on residential and commercial development in groundwater recharge watershed areas. The role of federal and state governments in these cases is instructive.

Long Island

The right of local governments to enact zoning laws to protect groundwater was challenged in Long Island. This case involved the rezoning of 11,000 acres within a critical recharge zone in eastern Suffolk County, Long Island, in the Town of Brookhaven. This rezoning increased the minimum lot size from quarter- and half-acre lots to two acres. Property owners challenged this in state and federal courts. Both courts upheld the validity of the rezoning and found no taking.[4] EDF was a party defendant in the federal court action.

The basic issue in both courts concerned the degree of land use controls which a local unit of government could invoke to protect the quality of its groundwater resources. Subsequent to the adoption of the Town of Brookhaven's 1975 Master Plan and the ordinance which incorporated the rezoning, the Long Island water quality management planning process under Section 208 of the Clean Water Act, 33 U.S.C. Section 1288, was initiated with a $5.2 million grant from EPA. The Long Island Regional Planning Board (LIRPB) and a number of consultants, together with cooperating Nassau and Suffolk County agencies, generated an enormous amount of hydrogeologic and water quality data, including toxicity data. These data were used to establish eight hydrogeologic zones each with its own groundwater (and surface water) management objectives (LIRPB, 1978). Brookhaven was therefore fortunate in the litigation in that it was able to rely on this 208 Plan and its hydrogeologic zoning framework which classified groundwater by quality class, levels of recharge areas, land use restrictions, and its water quality, impact assessments, and demographic data.

New Jersey Pine Barrens

New Jersey has an even more ambitious land use control program in a 1,100,000-acre groundwater recharge watershed area known as the Pine Barrens in southeastern New Jersey. This area represents the largest Pine Barrens in the world, and therefore a unique ecosystem of national, if not worldwide, importance. Pursuant to federal and state law, the State of New Jersey established a Pinelands Commission in 1979. That 15-member Commission, made up of seven Pineland county appointees, seven gubernatorial appointees, and a representative of the Secretary of Interior, prepared a Pinelands Comprehensive Management Plan. This Plan was approved by the Governor and the Secretary of Interior and went into effect in January 1981.[5]

---

4. See, <u>Omnia Properties v. Town of Brookhaven and EDF</u> (defendant intervenor), Dkt. No. 77C 574 (E.D.N.Y. Dec. 26, 1979); <u>Manorville 33 et al. v. The Town of Brookhaven</u>, <u>et al.</u>, Index No. 76-3639 (N.Y. Supreme Ct. Suffolk Co., May 10, 1979).

5. New Jersey Pinelands Comprehensive Management Plan (1980), prepared and adopted pursuant to Section 502 of the 1978 National Parks and Recreation Act, 16 U.S.C. Section 471i and the Pinelands Protection Act, 13 N.J.S.A. Section 13-18A-1.

While retaining overall population growth levels established by New Jersey's Department of Labor and Industry for the seven-county area, the Plan channels most of that anticipated growth away from the core 368,000-acre Preservation Area, Forest District Area, and Agricultural Production Areas into designated regional Growth Areas and Pinelands Villages and Towns. The Plan establishes stringent controls on residential and commercial development in the Preservation, Forest and Agricultural Production Areas. For example, in the Forest Area, average densities for new construction are in the range of one residential dwelling unit per 15 acres of privately held land.

The Plan also establishes a Pinelands Development credit program[6] which makes innovative and unprecedented use of a transfer-of-development-right strategy on a regional scale. While imposing stringent land use controls on these critical recharge watershed areas, the Plan awards Pinelands Development credits as "use rights" to landowners in the Preservation and Agricultural Production Areas. Developers of property in the Regional Growth Areas who intend to build to higher-than-base zoning densities, which local plans and zoning ordinances in conformity with the Plan prescribe, may purchase these credits for use as "bonus density" rights. Although litigation continues, the validity of the Pinelands Comprehensive Management Plan has been upheld in state and federal courts.[7]

In early 1982, Burlington County (the largest of the seven Pinelands counties) established an Exchange Board to buy and sell Pinelands Development credits and therefore facilitate exchange of these credits. Obviously, such an institutional mechanism can play a pivotal role in promoting this innovative program. When the Board announced its

---

6. New Jersey Pinelands Comprehensive Management Plan, supra, n. 5, pp. 210-212 and 401-402.

7. See, City of Brigantine v. Pinelands Commission, Superior Court of New Jersey, Appellate Division, Dkt.No. A-312-80 (motion for temporary restraining order against Preservation Area Plan denied Sept. 30, 1980); Township of Folsom v. State of New Jersey and Pinelands Commission, Superior Court of New Jersey, Appellate Division, Dkt. No. A-1675-80-T1 (following filing of all briefs, the court granted plaintiffs' motion to dismiss); Hovsons Inc. v. Secretary of Interior, 519 F. Supp. 434 (D.N.J. 1981), appeal pending, Dkt. No. 81-2580 (3rd Circuit).

intention to purchase its first credit, a county resident
immediately challenged the legality of the Board and its
proposed action in Burlington County Superior Court on several
grounds, including claims that the credits were securities for
purposes of the 1933 Securities Act and 1934 Securities
Exchange Act, and that federal and state law pre-empted the
county's action. The court denied the relief sought,
retaining jurisdiction over one factual issue: the[8]
reasonableness of the $10,000 purchase price of each credit.
Following a trial, the court found the purchase price to be
reasonable and therefore upheld the legality of this exchange
in all respects.[9]

Framework for National Groundwater Protection

An assessment of federal programs and local and state
planning efforts suggests several basic needs for effective
and complementary federal, state, and local groundwater
quality protection strategies. Without doubt, the country
must spend more money on groundwater quality research relating
to hydrogeology, health effects, and development of planning
tools for classification of groundwater and identification of
recharge zones. This need must be emphasized at a time when
the EPA research budget was cut back from $250 million to $180
million in fiscal year 1983. A federal policy should be
established to support state and local processes for
classifying groundwater, identifying objectives and standards,
preparing siting criteria, and identifying recharge zones and
appropriate land use controls. Such a policy should include
federal and local management programs, the provision for
transfer of development rights, a land credit exchange
program, and encouragement of resource utilization.

Management Programs

The federal government should establish a process to
facilitate local or state government programs to classify
groundwater, to select groundwater quality management
objectives for different aquifers based on their
classification framework, to identify land use control
programs designed to accomplish those policy objectives, and
to establish siting criteria for point and non-point sources

---

8. Matlack v. Board of Chosen Freeholders of the County of
    Burlington, Dkt. No. L-67582 D.W. (Sup. Ct. Burlington Co.
    Dec. 6, 1982).

9. Matlack v. Board of Chosen Freeholders, Dkt. No. L-67582-
    81 D.W. (Sup. Ct. Burlington Co., June 14, 1983).

of pollution.   Such a process should assist states and local
units of government in determining what their groundwater
quality goals are, what aquifers should be specifically
protected through land use controls over point and non-point
sources, what groundwater recharge areas may be used for
siting of hazardous waste facilities, and what alternatives to
land disposal of wastes must be promoted.

Transfer of Development Rights

At the state and local level where land use decisions are
made, local governments are constantly faced with claims that
the use of private property is unreasonably   restricted
whenever they make serious efforts to conserve natural
resources through zoning   changes.   Groundwater   quality
management planning in this country desperately needs
innovative experiments in institutionalizing what land use
planners call   transfer-of-development-right schemes as one
mechanism for controlling impacts of zoning changes on land
values and uses.   The experience with such transfer programs
in this country is exceedingly limited because of the lack of
traditional institutional mechanisms for transferring partial
rights in land and infrequent coordination among two or more
units of local government which may share a land resource,
such as a critical groundwater recharge watershed area.

Land Credit Exchange Program

Although the Comprehensive Management Plan for the New
Jersey Pine Barrens provides a land development credit
exchange scheme on the largest regional basis ever attempted
in this country, its efficient functioning is restrained by
the lack of an effective institutional exchange mechanism.
Aside from the Burlington County Exchange Board, no such
institution exists in the Pinelands to facilitate credit
exchanges.   Opponents of the Plan have opposed the
establishment of such a Pinelands institution.   A bill (A.
1259) is now before the New Jersey State Legislature to
establish a Pinelands Development credit exchange bank with
some initial state funding. A federal bill, S.1111 (H.R.79),
should give impetus to consideration and establishment of such
local and regional land credit exchange programs and
institutions to conserve critical recharge watershed land
resources.[10]

---

10. For a report which proposes the use of land credit
    exchange programs and other land use tools to conserve all
    112,000 acres of the remaining Pine Barrens of eastern
    Long Island and prohibit all development there as a

Resource Utilization

    In terms of long-term groundwater protection strategy in
the 1980´s, for both economic and environmental reasons,
industry must invest heavily in technologies and protection
techniques which affect the demand side of the hazardous waste
equation. A demand-side hazardous waste control investment
strategy is concerned with the sources of wastes and actions
to reduce the production, discharge or toxicity of wastes
through reuse, recycling, chemical or biological processes,
industrial process change, or tightly supervised and monitored
incineration. The Governor´s office in California has
completed a study entitled <u>Alternative to the Land Use
Disposal of Hazardous Wastes</u> (State of California, 1981; see
also Lueck, 1982). It suggests in California that the so-
called high priority wastes which now go to landfills and are
polluting groundwater could in fact be disposed of through
relatively benign means. The State of California Department
of Health Services has recently promulgated regulations which
phase out land disposal of[11] selected hazardous wastes as
alternatives become available.

    Considerable groundwater contamination in this decade
could come from energy development associated with synfuels,
mining, and disposal of brine and other wastes. In addition
to vigorous enforcement of the Surface Mining Control and
Reclamation Act, this observation simply means that all
efforts promoting energy conservation or efficient energy end
use will have a beneficial effect for groundwater quality.

    Subsurface disposal of residential wastes nationally is
also a major source of nitrate and toxic wastes. Although the
contribution from each residential system is small, the
cumulative impact is large. EPA should commit significant
groundwater protection research funds to development of a
subsurface system design capable of efficient denitrification
of these wastes. TOSCA can and should be used to impose
further restrictions on the use of solvents in homes with

---

    critical groundwater watershed, see <u>Watershed Planning for
the Protection of Long Island´s Groundwater</u> (Sept. 1982).

11. State of California Department of Health Services
    Regulations Regarding Hazardous Waste Land Disposal
    Restrictions, Refer. No. R-32-82 (Dec. 1982). These
    regulations ban the most troublesome wastes from land
    disposal in accordance with a schedule based on
    availability of alternatives.

subsurface disposal systems. Agriculture is another major pollution source for groundwater in some parts of the country, generating large amounts of nitrate and pesticide contaminants. If we look again at the demand side of the equation, incentives for integrated pest management would abate wasteful use of these contaminants, and in the process reduce opportunities for groundwater contamination.

In the 1980's, therefore, groundwater quality management strategies will benefit indirectly from demand-side resource utilization investments which will affect the volume and nature of industrial, agricultural, and residential waste.

Federal Legislation

While the Safe Drinking Water Act is up for reauthorization, Congress should expand its provisions to provide clear groundwater quality management objectives for identification and protection of critical recharge zones through controls on all federal, state, and county infrastructure projects and financially assisted activities. In addition, this program should establish a process for local or regional units of government to implement stringent land use controls within designated critical recharge zones.

A provision of the SDWA that has not been effectively exploited by either EPA or local communities is the Sole Source Aquifer designation program. The utility of this provision stems from its focus (unique among federal statutory provisions) on the recharge zone, implications of land uses in that zone for groundwater quality, and EPA's authority to review and veto federally assisted projects in that zone. Its present weakness stems from limits on EPA's federal project review authority, the lack of any comparable review over state or county infrastructure projects, a general ignorance about how to take advantage of a designation, EPA's unfortunate "endangerment" concept (42 Fed. Reg. 51,620,1977) [to be codified in 40 CFR Section 148.2 (j)] as the applicable standard for a groundwater quality standard (rather than a more powerful non-degradation standard), and as with all federal groundwater quality-related programs, the lack of any overall management objective.

Senator Moynihan has introduced a bill, S.1111, which is a significant step towards providing local, regional, and state governments with a tool for land use management. Under this bill, upon petition by a local government, the Governor of the state in question may designate boundaries of special protection areas (i.e., critical groundwater recharge

watershed areas) within larger areas which EPA has designated
under the Sole Source designation program [Section 1424(e) of
the SDWA]. The Governor may also establish a regional
planning entity responsible for preparing a plan with
appropriate land use controls preventing degradation of the
quality of groundwater recharged through the special
protection area. Under the bill, federal funds would be
available to support the planning enterprise on a cost-sharing
basis.

     Further, under S.1111, federal funds would be available
for land acquisition or, most important, as seed capital for a
land credit exchange institution (similar to that used by the
Burlington County Pine Barrens Exchange Board) to facilitate
transfer of credits representing partial interests in land so
that potential residential and commercial development in
watershed conservation areas may be transferred to designated
growth areas. Such a credit exchange system can both moderate
land value losses and gains in an equitable fashion which
zoning alone can seldom achieve. In the process, it could
provide a legal basis for outright prohibition on development
and maintenance of national vegetative systems, in the most
sensitive recharge watershed areas. Under the bill, state and
federal funds for these purposes would be available only if
the special protection area plan, as approved by the state and
EPA, were in fact implemented through appropriate changes in
local master plans and zoning ordinances.

Conclusion

     Throughout the 1970's, Congress enacted several laws
pertaining to surface water pollution. Although several of
these laws address segments of the groundwater pollution
problem, no comprehensive national program has been
established to regulate groundwater quality systematically.

     The first step in establishing any groundwater management
program is the classification of groundwater quality.
Aquifers may be divided into three classes: (1) those
containing pristine, high quality groundwater with recharge
areas that are largely unpolluted; (2) those in which some
contamination has occurred, but which remain potable with
reasonable treatment; and (3) those which are contaminated to
such an extent that they are unusable, or which are
hydrogeologically isolated. After identification of aquifer
quality, recharge areas should be identified and appropriate
land use restrictions imposed to prevent degradation of
groundwater quality. This implies that potential sites of
contamination be limited to recharge areas of the third class
of aquifers.

Such a national framework for classifying groundwater, identifying recharge areas, and prescribing land use controls based on recharge watershed conditions will provide for local and state groundwater protection strategies which are legally defensible from challenge. Further, it forms the basis for establishment of siting criteria for major point sources of groundwater pollution. Finally, a major component of a national groundwater quality protection program must be the search for and implementation of alternatives to land disposal of hazardous wastes. This surely requires a major scientific research effort by EPA, other agencies, and industry. Restitution and expansion of EPA's scientific research capability is essential to this end.

References

Council on Environmental Quality (CEQ). 1981. Contamination of Ground Water by Toxic Organic Chemicals. U.S. Government Printing Office, Washington, D.C.

Devine, M. D. and S. C. Ballard. 1982. Southern Regional Environmental Assessment: Environmental Status of the Sunbelt, University of Oklahoma Science and Public Policy Program Project, prepared for Office of Research and Development, U. S. Environmental Protection Agency.

Evans, D. D. and E. B. Frost. 1982. "Changes in Spill Liability Occasioned by the Passage of Superfund." pp. 321-324 in 1982 Hazardous Material Spills Conference Proceedings, April 19-22, 1982, Milwaukee, Wisconsin.

Gruson, K. 1983. "A Pesticide Too Good to Be True?" New York Times (April 24, 1983).

Harper, F. V. and F. James. 1956. The Law of Torts, Vol. I., Boston, Massachusetts.

Harris, D. and H. W. Davids. 1982. Report of the Occurrence and Movement of Agricultural Chemicals in Groundwater: South Fork of Suffolk County. Bureau of Water Resources, Suffolk County Department of Health Services, Long Island, N. Y.

Houk, V. H. 1982. "Determining the Impacts on Human Health Attributable to Hazardous Waste Sites." pp. 21-32 in Risk Assessment at Hazardous Waste Sites (F. A. Long and G. E. Schweitzer, eds.), Amer. Chem. Soc.

Long Island Regional Planning Board (LIRPB). 1978. The Long Island Comprehensive Waste Treatment Management Plan. (208 Study).

Lueck, T. J. 1982. "Technology - Toxic Waste Disposal," New York Times D3 (Thursday, Dec.30).

Mott, R. M. 1982. "Liability for Spill Cleanup: Legal Basis for Risk Assessment and Cost-Benefit Considerations." pp. 346-349 in 1982 Hazardous Material Spills Conference Proceedings, April 19-22, 1982, Milwaukee, Wisconsin.

Office of Technology Assessment (OTA). 1983. Technologies and Management Strategies for Hazardous Waste Control. U. S. Government Printing Office, Washington, D.C.

Prosser, Wade, Schwartz. 1976. Torts, Cases and Materials. University Casebook Series.

State of California. 1981. Alternatives to the Land Disposal of Hazardous Wastes, prepared by the Governor's Office of Appropriate Technology.

Tripp, J. T. B. 1976. "Coastal Zone Management: A Lawyer's Perspective." Time-Stressed Coastal Environments: Assessments and Future Action." Proceedings of the Second Annual Conference of the Coastal Society.

Tripp, J. T. B. and A. B. Jaffe. 1979. "Preventing Groundwater Pollution: Towards a Coordinated Strategy to Protect Critical Recharge Zones," Harv. Eng. L. (Rev. 1).

U. S. Environmental Protection Agency (EPA). 1977. Waste Disposal Practices and Their Effects on Groundwater. Report to Congress, U. S. Government Printing Office, Washington, D.C.